TABLE OF CONTENTS

GW01395811

Page

ILLUSTRATIONS

Page

CHAPTER 1

INTRODUCTION

This paper investigates the failure of British strategy in the American south from 1780 to 1781. The thesis of this research is that this failure was due to four factors: (1) a false British assumption of loyalist support among the local populace, (2) British application of self-defeating political and military policies, (3) the British failure to deploy sufficient forces to control the territory, and (4) patriot General Nathanael Greene's campaign against British forces. The chapters that follow examine each of these factors in detail.

In March 1778, King George III was eager to find a solution to what had become a political and military quagmire with the war in America. He established the Carlisle Peace Commission and dispatched the body to New York City with a proposal to cease hostilities. The American government insisted that the king and the British government agree to recognize American independence. The commission refused to make this concession and both parties recognized that they had arrived at an impasse.

Faced with this intractable problem, British Prime Minister Lord Frederick North came under intense political pressure to achieve a military breakthrough. The Secretary of State for the American Department, Lord George Germain, was the official directly responsible to the government for British performance in the war. After Carlisle's failure, Germain wrote that the opposition Whig Party in Parliament might make it "almost impossible to the present Ministry to remain in office."[1] Therefore, he worked fervently to develop a new strategy to demonstrate to the Parliament and king that victory was still attainable. Germain came to believe that southern loyalists were prepared to rise up in great numbers to defeat the rebels if British troops provided them protection. To acquire a sufficient number of troops to protect the loyalists, Germain used traditional recruiting techniques such as hiring mercenaries from the state of Hesse-Cassel, impressing criminals convicted by the courts, and offering bounties to volunteers.

On 8 March 1778, Germain sent a letter to General Henry Clinton, commander in chief of all British forces in North America, declaring that conquering the southern states of Georgia, South Carolina, and North Carolina was absolutely essential. Germain wrote that this was "considered by the King as an object of great importance in the scale of the war."[2] He believed that Great Britain should isolate the active center of the American rebellion in New England by invading the south. This would damage the rebels' economic base by depriving them of the revenue they generated by exporting southern crops such as rice, indigo, and tobacco. The American government used the funds from these crops to purchase war stocks and equipment from Europe. Germain gave Clinton broad latitude in planning the invasion of the south. He wrote, "Your own knowledge of those provinces, and the information you can collect from the naval and military officers that have been upon service there, will enable you to give the officer to whom you may entrust the command better instructions than I can pretend to point out to you at this distance."[3]

On 12 May 1780, patriot General Benjamin Lincoln surrendered his entire 5,500-man army to Clinton at Charleston, South Carolina in the greatest American disaster of the war. Three months later, General Charles Cornwallis and his 2,200-man army won a crushing victory over General Horatio Gates and his 4,100 American troops at the Battle of Camden, South Carolina. The British killed or wounded 800 of Gates's soldiers and captured 1,000. The remnants of the American army fled north to Charlotte and Hillsborough, North Carolina in disarray. It appeared that the British had solidified their position of complete dominance over the south.

Yet only seven months later, Cornwallis permanently abandoned the southern backcountry and took refuge with his army along the coast at Wilmington, North Carolina. Six months after that, patriot General Nathanael Greene engaged the last remaining contingent of British forces in the southern backcountry at the Battle of Eutaw Springs on 8 September 1781. Afterwards, the British commander, Lieutenant Colonel Alexander Stewart, withdrew his forces to Charleston, fifty miles to the southwest. The British never ventured into the southern backcountry again and their last remaining garrisons were the coastal bases at Wilmington, Charleston, and Savannah. In a period of 13 months, British forces in the south had gone from what appeared to be complete mastery of the territory to complete abandonment of it.

Germain's strategy for the south was to rally the support of the local populace for British rule. His goal was to use British military power to protect loyalist militias while they organized and rose up in great numbers to defeat the rebels. He also wanted these loyalists to provide aid and logistical support to British forces throughout the backcountry. The following chapters examine the failure of this strategy.

Chapter 2 examines the false British assumption of widespread loyalist support in the south. It surveys the key British political and military leaders who were instrumental in the origin of Lord Germain's strategy. It also explores the influence of existing patriot and loyalist sentiment throughout the south and the nature of the populace.

Chapter 3 focuses on a number of self-defeating British political and military policies. These include General Clinton's failure to reestablish civilian government in the south following his capture of Charleston. It also includes his decision to withdraw his support for neutrality among the southern populace. Following that, this chapter explores the failure of British commanders to convince local leaders to join the loyalist cause. Next, it focuses on British and loyalist atrocities against patriot forces and civilians. Lastly, it analyzes British policy on slavery and Indians.

Chapter 4 examines the British failure to deploy sufficient forces to control the south and protect southern loyalists. It explores the reasons behind Great Britain's attempt to accomplish this difficult task with a 4,000-man army. Next, it surveys patriot militia battlefield success against British and loyalist forces throughout the southern backcountry during the second half of 1780. Lastly, it analyzes the patriot militia victory over loyalist forces led by Major Patrick Ferguson at the Battle of King's Mountain on 7 October 1780.

Chapter 5 focuses on General Nathanael Greene's campaign against British forces in the south. This chapter examines his use of mobile warfare against Cornwallis's army. Next, it explores Greene's effectiveness in rallying the support of local leaders. Following that, this chapter analyzes his use of patriot militias against British forces. Additionally, it examines Greene's battles with the British at Cowpens and Guilford Courthouse and Cornwallis's permanent withdrawal from the backcountry in April 1781. Lastly, it surveys Greene's final battles to destroy British backcountry garrisons during the remainder of 1781.

A number of scholars have written works on the American Revolutionary War in the south. In 1962, William B. Willcox produced *Portrait of a General: Sir Henry Clinton in the War of Independence*. This is the definitive biography of the general. Willcox draws on numerous primary sources, including Clinton's private papers, to analyze the general's decisions and policies. He also examines Clinton's difficult relationships with Germain and Cornwallis. Lastly, Willcox describes Clinton's challenges as commander in chief of all British forces in North America.

In 1964, Piers Mackesy's *The War for America, 1775-1783* appeared. This book is an important contribution to the historical record. It describes British military operations in North America in the context of the broader conflict with France, Spain, and Holland. Mackesy clearly addresses the formidable operational and logistical problems that the British faced. He examines their difficulties in raising, maintaining, and supplying an army across 3,000 miles of ocean in an era of sailing ships and limited governmental powers.

Franklin and Mary Wickwire's *Cornwallis: The American Adventure* was published in 1970. Mr. Wickwire is the definitive modern biographer of Lord Cornwallis and this work covers the general's experiences during the war in America. Other works by Wickwire on the same topic include *Cornwallis and the War of Independence* published in 1971 and *Cornwallis: The Imperial Years* published in 1980. In *Cornwallis: The American Adventure*, the author sites numerous primary sources and follows the general's rise to command all British forces in the south. He also examines Cornwallis's difficult relationship with General Henry Clinton and his personal observations from his battles with Greene's patriot army.

John S. Pancake produced *This Destructive War: The British Campaign in the Carolinas, 1780-1782* in 1985. He describes in great detail the factors that led to violence between southern patriots and loyalists. Pancake argues that the failure of British strategy was due to counterproductive military action. He also asserts that the British failed to tie tactical victories on the battlefield to a sound strategy.

Christopher Hibbert's *Redcoats and Rebels: The American Revolution Through British Eyes* appeared in 1990. Hibbert analyzes Great Britain's increasing logistical difficulties in supporting campaigns against North America, France, and Spain. He identifies French intervention as an essential element of American victory. Hibbert also provides an excellent description of the social and political factors that led to the British battles at Savannah, Charleston, and King's Mountain.

In 1997, John Buchanan produced *The Road to Guilford Courthouse: The American Revolution in the Carolinas*. This work is a detailed account of British engagements with southern rebels. Buchanan provides insight into the social and economic factors that were critical to the rise of the patriot militias. He also references key primary sources and provides important quotes by commanders.

Walter B. Edgar's *Partisans and Redcoats: The Southern Conflict that Turned the Tide of the American Revolution* was published in 2001. The author describes a number of atrocities committed by British and loyalist forces against civilians and patriot militias in the south. Edgar argues that these atrocities mobilized the local populace against the British. He also describes the propaganda campaign that both sides waged to manipulate the attitudes of the local populace.

Although British political and military leaders agreed that conquering the south was a crucial goal during the American war, there was a great deal of confusion and disagreement about how to achieve that goal. This confusion and disagreement set the stage for a bloody, violent campaign that involved regular forces and militias and ranged from battlefields to private homes. This research demonstrates that there were clear factors that contributed to Great Britain's failure to rally the support of the local populace in the south in 1780 and 1781.

---

[1] John S. Pancake, *This Destructive War: The British Campaign in the Carolinas, 1780-1782* (Tuscaloosa: University of Alabama Press, 1985), 27.

[2] Pancake, 29-30.

[3] Henry Steele Commager and Richard B. Morris, eds., *The Spirit of Seventy Six: The Story of the American Revolution as Told by Participants* (New York: Da Capo Press, 1995), 1075.

CHAPTER 2

FALSE ASSUMPTION

One of the four factors that led to the failure of British strategy in the south during 1780 and 1781 was Lord George Germain's false assumption of widespread loyalist support. This chapter surveys the key British political and military leaders who influenced Germain's strategy. It also explores patriot and loyalist sentiment throughout the south and the nature of the populace. Because Lord Germain based his strategy on a false assumption of widespread southern loyalists, it was flawed at inception. This led directly to the strategy's failure.

The French and Indian War began as a colonial territorial dispute between England and France in North America in the early 1750s. It soon initiated a chain of events that spread around the world. In 1756, Prussia invaded Saxony. In 1757, the Holy Roman Empire declared war on Prussia and Prussia countered by invading Bohemia. England, France, Spain, and Russia all deployed forces based on a complex array of alliances and secret treaties. This conflict became known as the Seven Years' War and the participants fought more than 30 major battles in Europe, North America, India, the Philippines, and Cuba.

Although the outcome of the French and Indian War was virtually assured with the French surrender of Quebec in 1759, the fighting went on in North America, primarily between the British and Indians. On 10 February 1763, the Treaty of Paris officially ended the French and Indian War and the Seven Years' War. However, Great Britain now labored under massive debt incurred by Prime Minister William Pitt's policy of heavy borrowing to finance the war. To make the American colonies pay for their defense and alleviate the crushing debt, George III imposed a series of taxes against the colonies. These new taxes began with the Navigation Acts, which the government changed from a tool of trade regulation to revenue production. The new taxes eventually contributed to open rebellion by the American colonists.

During this difficult and complex period, Great Britain needed a strong, unified government. The king and Parliament produced political chaos instead. Pitt opposed George III's new taxes and the king dismissed him in 1761. He replaced Pitt with Lord Bute. However, Parliament did not accept Bute and forced his resignation in 1763. Bute was followed by Prime Minister Grenville, who was replaced by Rockingham, who was soon replaced by the return of Pitt (now the Earl of Chatham). Following Pitt's retirement, George III kept the position of prime minister open for almost two years hoping for his return. Pitt returned to office briefly, only to retire permanently to become a member of the opposition Whig Party.[1]

Finally, in 1770, George III installed Lord Frederick North as first lord of the treasury and prime minister. North had previously served as lord of the treasury, paymaster general, and chancellor of the exchequer. He would serve as prime minister for the next twelve years. With Lord George Germain as his Secretary of State for the American Department, North played a crucial role in implementing Great Britain's southern strategy in 1780 and 1781.

Lord North's Ministry was composed of the cabinet and the secretaries of state. The cabinet developed and approved policy and the secretaries issued orders to department heads. North presided over the cabinet while also serving as prime minister and first lord of the treasury. Within the ministry, three secretaries of state administered three separate departments. The Secretaries of State for the Northern and Southern Departments administered policy over British operations in northern and southern Europe, respectively. North created the office of secretary of state for the American department in 1772. The American Secretary was responsible for operations in the West Indies and North America. Between five and seven chief ministers typically joined North at cabinet meetings. These included the three secretaries of state, the first lord of the admiralty, the commander in chief, the lord privy seal, the lord president of the council, and the lord chancellor.[2]

George III was committed to returning the American colonies to British rule. By selecting Lord North as prime minister and surrounding himself with other Tory ministers, the political divide between the king and the opposition Whig Party in Parliament became increasingly wide. George III refused to consult with leaders of the Whig Party, although many of them wielded great influence with the British people. This was crucial in 1777 and 1778 as the king's Whig opponents reflected the populace's growing distrust of the government's handling of the war.

This distrust reached a critical point after a series of blows to the British war effort in the late 1770s. These included American General Horatio Gates's stunning defeat of British General John Burgoyne and his 5,000-man army at Saratoga, New York in October 1777; ratification of the formal alliance between France and the United States in May 1778; and the declaration of war between England and France in June 1778. These events strengthened Whig political power in Parliament and increased the king's frustration. George III wrote about his dislike for the Whigs, "Honestly, I would rather lose the crown I now wear than bear the ignominy of possessing it under their shackles . .

10

. no consideration in life will make me stoop to Opposition . . . it is impossible that the nation will not stand by me . . . if they will not, they shall have another King."[3]

As prime minister, Lord North proved ill-suited to leading the bureaucracy of the British Empire in time of war. He entered the House of Commons at the age of 22 and quickly rose to prominence. North's peers described him as easy-going, good-natured, and a "man of general knowledge, of a versatile understanding, fitted for every sort of business, of infinite wit and pleasantry, of a delightful temper."[4] Although North was a brilliant politician, he appeared awkward and clumsy. One of North's contemporaries wrote that he had "two large prominent eyes that rolled about to no purpose (for he was utterly short sighted). A wide mouth, thick lips, and inflated visage gave him the air of a blind trumpeter."[5]

Although North was a skillful politician and a brilliant economist, he was a military amateur. He wrote, "Upon military matters I speak ignorantly and without effect."[6] As the war progressed, North became increasingly isolated from his cabinet and emotionally depressed. He pleaded with George III to allow him to retire and wrote to the king, "Your Majesty's service requires a man of great abilities, and who is confident of his abilities, who can choose decisively, and carry his determination authoritatively into execution. . . . I am certainly not such a man."[7]

Surprisingly, George III agreed with North's self-assessment. However, he preferred to retain North as an ineffective prime minister rather than go through the difficult political process of replacing him. The king wrote that North's "irresolution is only to be equaled by a certain vanity of wanting to ape the Prime Minister without any of the requisite qualities."[8] While acknowledging North's failure as a strategist, George

11

III continued to press him for competent administration of the ministry. He wrote that North "must cast off his indecision and bear up, or no plan can succeed; he must be more exact in answering letters or let others do it for him; and he must let matters be thoroughly canvassed before undertaken, and when adopted must not quit them."[9]

North was the unhappy beneficiary of prevailing political thought following the end of the Seven Years' War. General Thomas Dundas and William Pitt argued that finance had become the decisive element in warfare, that "all modern wars are a contention of the purse, and the war minister should be the Minister of Finance."[10] Although the British constitution did not specify that the first lord of the treasury must also serve as prime minister, this was the unfortunate and unwanted position that North found himself in for twelve years. The king and Parliament expected North to administer the government, manage its financial affairs, oversee the affairs of state, and develop a strategy to win the war in North America. To accomplish this, North's Ministry maintained direct operational control over the British Army.

Unlike the army, the Royal Navy maintained a great deal of independence in government. John Montagu, fourth Earl of Sandwich, served as first lord of the admiralty in North's Ministry. Sir John Fortescue described Sandwich as "a politician of evil reputation and an inveterate jobber."[11] Secretaries rarely transmitted operational orders directly to British admirals as they did regularly to British generals. Instead, they sent their orders to the navy through Sandwich, who passed them to the board of admiralty, who then issued the orders to the admirals afloat.[12] In this way, the Royal Navy maintained a degree of independence from cabinet control that the army was unable to achieve. This distinction became critical as Germain developed his new strategy for employing British military power in the south.

Lord George Germain was born George Sackville and served as a lieutenant general in the British Army during the Seven Year' War. During that conflict, Sackville assumed command of British forces serving in Germany under Prince Ferdinand of Brunswick. At the Battle of Minden, Ferdinand's staff reported that Sackville was slow to obey orders to attack with his cavalry. Ferdinand accused Sackville of cowardice and reprimanded him. The British commander in chief dismissed Sackville from the army upon his return to England. However, it is not clear whether the charge of cowardice was legitimate. Prior to the battle, Ferdinand and Sackville had argued over Ferdinand's decision to abandon the town of Munster during the campaign. It was rumored that Ferdinand may have levied the charge of cowardice against Germain out of spite.

Sackville demanded and received a court martial in March 1760. The court found him not guilty of cowardice, but guilty of disobedience. Seven of the fifteen officers of the court voted for death, but they could not carry out the sentence without a two-thirds majority. The court ruled that Sackville was "unfit to serve His Majesty in any military capacity" and the elderly George II ordered the judgment read out to every regiment in the British Army. The court's judgment was an appalling disgrace for Sackville and his political enemies referred to him as "The Coward of Minden" for the rest of his life.[13]

Fortunately for Sackville, conditions changed dramatically in a short period of time. Six months after his court martial, George II was dead. Soon afterwards, the 22-year-old George III ascended the throne. The new king was determined to break the power of the great Whig families that had ruled England since 1714 and chose

Sackville's political friend Lord Bute as prime minister. Sackville's rehabilitation was underway. After fighting a duel with a Whig member of Parliament and inheriting a fortune from Lady Elizabeth Germain, Sackville changed his name to George Germain and his political rehabilitation was complete. Horace Walpole was one of Germain's contemporaries in Parliament. He wrote that Lord George Germain had "become a hero, whatever Lord George Sackville may have been."[14]

Germain's hostile rhetoric towards the Americans soon brought him to the attention of George III. The king found Germain to be a like-minded Tory politician and he appointed Germain Secretary of State for the American Department in 1775. One of Germain's contemporaries reported that he was a "tall man with a long face, rather strong features, clear blue eyes . . . and a mixture of quickness and a sort of melancholy in his look that runs through all the Sackville family."[15] There was also a widespread belief that Germain was homosexual. Germain's political enemies spread rumors throughout Parliament insinuating this for years.

One particularly vicious rumor involved Germain's supposed homosexual relationship with a young American loyalist named Benjamin Thompson. Germain took Thompson into his home in 1778 and made him under secretary of his department in 1780.[16] Reverend Percival Stockdale wrote that Germain's personality "depressed and darkened all that was agreeable and engaging in him. . . . His integrity commanded esteem, his abilities praise; but to attract the heart was not one of those abilities."[17]

Following Burgoyne's surrender at Saratoga in 1777 and France's entry into the war in 1778, North and Germain recognized that the political goals of the war had to be lowered. Although the situation was desperate, the king was not ready to admit defeat. He wrote, "America cannot now be deserted without the loss of the Islands [West Indies]; therefore we must stretch every nerve to defend ourselves, and must run risks; if we are to play the cautious game ruin will inevitably ensue."[18]

In March 1778, George III approved the formation and dispatch of the Carlisle Peace Commission to North America. The commission was named for its chairman, Frederick Howard, fifth Earl of Carlisle. The king granted Lord Carlisle the authority to negotiate directly with Congress and to offer the suspension of any act of Parliament passed since 1763. With the British evacuating Philadelphia and the Americans confident of French support, Congress was not interested in negotiating any measure short of total British withdrawal. On 22 April 1778, Congress resolved that any individual or group that came to an agreement with the Carlisle Commission was an enemy of the United States and negotiations broke down. Carlisle resorted to bribery and offered royal pardons to a number of individual congressmen. This effectively ended negotiations and the Marquis de Lafayette challenged Carlisle to a duel for defaming France in letters to Congress, although no duel was ever fought.

Back in Parliament, Carlisle's failure gave the leaders of the Whig Party an ideal opportunity to criticize North and Germain. In the House of Commons, Charles Fox declared that North and Germain were guilty of "want of policy, of folly and madness." Fox labeled North a "blundering pilot who had brought the nation into its present difficulties. . . . Alexander the Great never gained more in one campaign than the noble Lord [North] has lost--he has lost a whole continent."[19] The London Chronicle described Fox's speech as "masterly, forcible, and expressive" with the "most striking proofs of judgment, sound reasoning and astonishing memory."[20]

15

During Whig strategy meetings, the party leaders developed a careful plan of attack. They did not want to appear joyful about British misfortune in North America in 1777 and 1778, although it was admittedly to their political benefit. Lord Rockingham wrote that the Whigs resolved to be "manly and firm" and planned to expose "how the public had been deceived and misled" by North and Germain.[21] Lord Chatham, formerly William Pitt, unleashed a scathing attack in the House of Lords:

> No man thinks more highly than I of the virtue and valour of British troops; I know they can achieve anything except impossibilities; and the conquest of English America is an impossibility. You cannot, I venture to say it, you cannot conquer America. . . . What is your present situation there? We do not know the worst, but we know that in three campaigns we have done nothing, and suffered much. . . . Conquest is impossible: you may swell every expense and every effort still more extravagantly; pile and accumulate every assistance you can buy or borrow; traffic and barter with every pitiful German prince that sells his subjects to the shambles of a foreign power; your efforts are forever vain and impotent; doubly so from this mercenary aid on which you rely; for it irritates to an incurable resentment the minds of your enemies. . . . If I were an American, as I am an Englishman, while a foreign troop was landed in my country, I would never lay down my arms, never, never, never![22]

In this tense atmosphere of accusation and counteraccusation, Germain began to pay attention to a treasury officer named Charles Jenkinson. Jenkinson argued that New England could be sacrificed without significant damage to British security or trade. He reasoned that Great Britain had no need to control New England's commerce and that only southern tobacco was worth regulating with restrictive trade tariffs. Jenkinson believed that New Englanders would continue to buy British wool and hardware due to low prices, regardless of the war. He also believed that invading the south would only damage the British linen trade, which was acceptable. Jenkinson argued that by invading the south, the government could still achieve military victory in America and maintain its international prestige. He wrote, "If I should happen to be right, how much mistaken and deluded have been the people of this country for more than a century past."[23]

Under Secretary for the American Department William Knox took this argument even further. He wrote two letters critical of the past strategy of the war. He argued that the government had failed because the army attacked the Americans where they were strongest, in New England and the north. Knox agreed with Jenkinson that the army should invade the south and conquer Georgia, South Carolina, and North Carolina. He wrote that this would put tremendous pressure on the rebels in Virginia by placing the British Army to their south, the Royal Navy on the coast to their east, and Great Britain's Indian and loyalist allies to their west.[24]

Germain found this argument compelling. He based his new strategy of rallying the support of the southern populace on Knox's argument. He described the strategy in 1778: "The great point to be wished for, is that the inhabitants of some considerable colony were so far reclaimed to their duty, that the revival of the British Constitution, and the free operation of the laws, might without prejudice be permitted amongst them." In this way "a little political management, would with ease bring about what will never be effected by mere force."[25] This strategy was based on Germain's assumption of widespread loyalist sentiment throughout the south. Although many senior officials in the North Ministry shared this belief, it was false.

A number of those officials played a key role in influencing Germain's beliefs. General James Robertson insisted that the southern loyalists were simply waiting for the British Army to provide the help that would "enable the loyal subjects of America to get free from the tyranny of the rebels."[26] South Carolina Attorney General James Simpson reported that "whenever the King's troops move to Carolina they will be assisted by a very considerable number of the inhabitants."[27] Royal Governors James Wright of Georgia and William Campbell of South Carolina wrote, "From our particular knowledge of those two provinces, it appears very clear to us that if a proper number of troops were in possession of Charleston . . . the whole inhabitants of both provinces would soon come in and submit."[28]

Another advocate of the southern loyalist strategy was renegade American congressman Joseph Galloway. He maintained a good deal of affection towards Great Britain and evacuated Philadelphia with British forces in June 1778. Following his departure, Galloway sailed to England and wrote a series of letters indicating that southern loyalists were waiting expectantly for the British Army to invade. He wrote that upon the arrival of British troops, the loyalists would "disarm the rebel minority by their own efforts."[29] General Robertson endorsed Galloway's assessment and wrote, "It is on this foundation that we should build our hopes."[30]

At this time, relations between North and Germain were strained. Germain was already convinced of the southern loyalist strategy and he presented Galloway and Robertson's arguments to North as supporting evidence. He realized that if North believed that he had developed the strategy alone, he would disapprove it. Germain wrote to Knox of his ideas, "If he [North] adopts them, they may be of use; if they come only from me, I know their fate."[31] Germain's plan was successful and North authorized him to implement the southern strategy. Germain quickly dispatched orders to General Henry Clinton, commander in chief of all British forces in North America. He wrote, "The recovery of the southern provinces, and the prosecution of the war by pushing our conquests from south to north, is to be considered as the chief and principal object for the employment of all forces under your command."[32]

Germain and North clearly accepted the idea of widespread loyalists in the south. However, conditions had not much changed there since North Carolina Royal Governor Josiah Martin attempted to defeat what he called the "monster of sedition" that had "dared to raise his impious head in America" in 1775.[33] Martin distributed 10,000 muskets, six-pound cannons, and supplies to Highland Scots in North Carolina. He ordered an elderly Scotsman named Donald MacDonald to lead an expedition to track down the patriot militias that had begun operating in the south. Martin assumed that British troops promised by Germain's predecessor, Lord Dartmouth, would support his loyalists during the campaign. This proved to be a false assumption.

The southern patriots were well organized and prepared for Martin's loyalists. By 1775, rebel leaders had succeeded in establishing six committees of safety in North Carolina. The First Continental Congress approved these committees and they quickly spread throughout the colonies. They were the primary means by which local patriots organized militia units and obtained pledges of support from local leaders.

On 18 February 1776, MacDonald led his 1,580 loyalist troops out of Cross Hill, North Carolina southeast towards the coast in search of rebel militias. Learning of MacDonald's approach, the New Bern Committee of Safety chose patriot militia Colonel Richard Caswell to lead an expedition to destroy the loyalists. In Wilmington, patriot leaders selected Colonel Alexander Lillington to lead their militia forces. In addition, Colonel James Moore had begun searching for MacDonald with his 1,100 patriot militia. Moore assumed overall command of the rebels and defeated MacDonald at the Battle of

Moore's Creek Bridge on 27 February 1776, capturing MacDonald and killing 30 loyalists.

In a pattern that was repeated throughout the war in the south, the rebels released the majority of the captured loyalists on parole after they swore loyalty oaths. Governor Martin's plan to defeat the southern rebellion and rally the loyalists was in shambles. After the battle, the *New York Packet* predicted, "this, we think, will effectively put a stop to Toryism in North Carolina."[34] While this prediction was not completely accurate, the outcome of the Battle of Moore's Creek Bridge did suppress loyalist sentiment in the south for years to follow. North and Germain did not understand that this type of small engagement between loyalists and patriots greatly influenced public opinion in the south.

The British Commander in Chief in North America was General Henry Clinton. He succeeded General William Howe on 8 May 1778. One of Clinton's staff officers described him as "an honorable and respectable officer of the German school; having served under Prince Ferdinand of Prussia and the Duke of Brunswick. Vain, open to flattery; and from a great aversion to all business not military, too often misled by aides de camp and favourites."[35] Clinton did not share Germain's belief in the widespread existence of southern loyalists. He wrote, "there does not exist in any one [province] in America a number of friends of Government sufficient to defend themselves when the troops are withdrawn. The idea is false and if the measure is adopted . . . all the friends of Government will be sacrificed *en detail*. This is the case in Georgia, will be in South Carolina, is already in North Carolina . . . and must in my opinion be everywhere."[36]

Clinton's relationship with his fellow officers and his political superiors was extremely strained. He spent much of his time writing reports requesting more troops and demanding to be left alone. He wrote to Germain in May 1779, "For God's sake, my Lord, if you wish me to do anything, leave me to myself and let me adapt my efforts to the hourly change of circumstances."[37] In a letter challenging Germain on his belief in the strength of southern loyalists he wrote, "Why, my Lord, without consulting me you will adopt the ill digested or interested suggestions of people who cannot be competent judges of the subject, and puzzle me by hinting wishes with which I cannot agree but am loath to disregard."[38] Neither was Germain fond of Clinton. He wrote that Clinton behaved "more from caprice than from common sense. . . . When we act with such a man, we must be cautious not to give him any opportunity of doing a rash action under the sanction of what he may call a positive order."[39]

Following Clinton's capture of Charleston on 12 May 1780, he appointed General Charles Cornwallis as his commander in the south. Cornwallis had developed an excellent reputation within the British Army. One of Cornwallis's staff officers described him as "a good officer, devoted to the service of his country . . . beloved by the army."[40] Germain's nephew described Cornwallis as "deservedly the favourite of every person of every rank under his command."[41]

Clinton and Cornwallis's relationship became increasingly strained after Lincoln's surrender at Charleston. Clinton was aware that Cornwallis's ambition was to succeed him as commander in chief and that Cornwallis was more popular with the army than he was. This gave rise to jealousy and mistrust and led to a gradual breakdown in communication. Clinton wrote of Cornwallis, "I can never be cordial with such a man" and "whenever he is with me, there are symptoms that I do not like."[42]

In a surprising move, Cornwallis asked for a separate command after Clinton captured Charleston. By doing so, Cornwallis was attempting to place himself and his troops directly under Germain's operational control and cut Clinton out of his chain of command. Clinton took this as a mortal insult. Not surprisingly, he was furious. Clinton departed Charleston in June 1778 and returned to New York, leaving Cornwallis in command of all British forces in the south. Clinton wrote, "I leave Cornwallis here with sufficient force to keep [Charleston] against the world, without a superior fleet shows itself, in which case I shall despair of ever seeing peace restored to this miserable country."[43] The damaged relationship between Clinton and Cornwallis's led to a breakdown in communication between the two officers. This later contributed to Cornwallis's isolation as the southern campaign gradually reduced his army's effectiveness in 1780 and 1781.

Adding to this serious communication problem between the military commanders, Germain had failed to consider the nature of the southern populace when developing his strategy. The south was a politically divided region. Animosity among the inhabitants was a product of southern geography; various long-running religious, ethnic, and territorial disputes; and widely divergent political ideologies. These factors explain why Cornwallis found pockets of strong British support in some southern communities and strong patriot support in others.

Wealthy southern families along the coast managed large slave plantations or engaged in maritime trade. The most prominent plantation owners were known throughout the region as Rice Kings. They were most directly affected by British economic policy and were most likely to support the rebellion. They also dominated the local government. In the backcountry, many Scotch-Irish Presbyterians established farms and raised livestock. They often viewed the rebellious Rice Kings as arrogant aristocrats who were not much different from the British they opposed. Many of the Scotch-Irish identified more closely with the British government and were more likely to become loyalists.

Reverend Charles Woodmason wrote that the southern backcountry was populated by Lutheran Germans, French Huguenots, Baptists, Seventh Day Baptists, New Light Baptists, and "an hundred other sects." Many of the Germans received their land directly from the British authorities. Most of these immigrants wanted no part in the rebellion because they were fearful of losing their farms. They mostly wanted both sides to leave them alone so they could grow their crops and tend their animals. Former South Carolina Royal Governor William Bull described the southern religious and ethnic groups as "subdivided ad infinitum in the back parts, as illiterate enthusiasm or wild imagination can misinterpret the scripture" while "every circle of Christian knowledge grows fainter as more removed from the center."[44]

Local religious leaders influenced political sentiment in the south. In their sermons, many of these men preached against British injustice. Reverend William Martin exhorted his South Carolina congregation, "My hearers, talk and angry words will do no good. We must fight!" Gesturing towards the location of a recent backcountry battle, Martin said, "Go see the tender mercies of Great Britain! In that church you may find men, though still alive, hacked out of the very semblance of humanity; some deprived of their arms, some with one arm or leg, and some with both legs cut off. Is not this cruelty a parallel to the history of our Scottish fathers?"[45] Congregation member William

23

Anderson decided to join the rebellion based on Reverend Martin's sermon. Martin convinced him that British tyranny in the south had become intolerable. Anderson wrote, "The way is now clear; the word of God approves."[46]

Other southern religious leaders went further. They viewed the revolution as a holy war between the forces of Christ and Antichrist that would bring about the millennium. Reverend Samuel Mather preached against the presence of Great Britain's "profane" legions in America and claimed that God had "sanctified" the rebels.[47] Many of these leaders told their congregations that killing British soldiers was a religious duty. They preached that if a man joined the rebellion, then he would "escape the bondage of his soul to sin."[48]

Another aspect of southern culture that escaped Lord Germain was how frequently the loyalists and patriots changed sides. This was not limited to individuals or even militia units. Entire communities occasionally switched from one side to the other, depending upon who was strongest in their local area at the moment. A good example is Georgetown, South Carolina. Following Clinton's capture of Charleston, the community leaders wrote, "The original cause of the disputes between Great Britain and her colonies" over taxation had been resolved by one of Clinton's policies. "We are therefore desirous of becoming British Subjects in which capacity we promise to behave ourselves with all becoming fidelity and loyalty."[49] The residents of Georgetown had abandoned the rebellion in favor of the British Army, which dominated the coastal region.

A common example of militias changing sides occurred at the Battle of Camden in August 1780. When local patriot militias learned of Cornwallis's victory, they simply switched sides, declared their allegiance to Great Britain, and attacked their former friends. Patriot Colonel Otho Williams described what happened to a group of North

Carolina militiamen as they attempted to escape from the battlefield: "They met many of

their insidious friends, armed, and advancing to join the American army; but learning its

fate from the refugees, they acted decidedly in concert with the victors; and, captivating

some, plundering others, and maltreating all the fugitives they met, returned, exultingly,

home."[50]

It is unlikely that Lord Germain considered these aspects of southern culture as he

was developing his strategy. His false belief in the widespread existence of southern

loyalists led directly to the failure of his strategy. Clinton wrote prophetically of

Germain, "His Lordship seemed also to have cherished very sanguine ideas of the great

number of loyalists I should be enabled to embody in the provincial corps."[51]

Chapter 3 explores the self-defeating British political and military policies that

contributed to the failure Lord Germain's strategy in 1780 and 1781. These include

General Clinton's failure to reestablish civilian government following his capture of

Charleston. The chapter analyzes Clinton's decision to withdraw his support for

neutrality among the southern populace. Following that, it examines the failure of British

commanders to convince local leaders to join the loyalist cause. Next, it focuses on

British and loyalist atrocities against rebels and civilians. Lastly, it analyzes British

policy on slavery and Indians.

---

[1]Mark M. Boatner III, *Encyclopedia of the American Revolution* (Mechanicsburg, Pennsylvania: Stackpole Books, 1994), 219-220.

[2]Piers Mackesy, *The War for America, 1775-1783* (Lincoln, Nebraska: University of Nebraska Press, 1993), 12-13.

[3]Christopher Hibbert, *Redcoats and Rebels: The American Revolution Through*

British Eyes (New York: W. W. Norton & Company, 2002), 204.

[4]Ibid.,17.

[5]Ibid.,18.

[6]Mackesy, 21.

[7]Hibbert, 204.

[8]Mackesy, 23.

[9]Ibid., 24.

[10]Ibid., 21.

[11]Boatner, 969.

[12]Mackesy, 16.

[13]Ibid., 49.

[14]Hibbert, 86.

[15]Ibid., 87.

[16]Mackesy, 51.

[17]Ibid.

[18]John S. Pancake, *This Destructive War: The British Campaign in the Carolinas, 1780-1782* (Tuscaloosa: University of Alabama Press, 1985), 27.

[19]Hibbert, 86.

[20]Ibid., 203.

[21]Ibid., 202.

[22]Ibid.

[23]Mackesy, 158-159.

[24]Ibid., 158.

[25]Pancake, 12.

[26]Ibid., 29.

[27]Ibid., 29-30.

[28]Dan L. Morrill, *Southern Campaigns of the American Revolution* (Baltimore: The Nautical & Aviation Publishing Company of America, 1993), 39.

[29]Mackesy, 253.

[30]Ibid., 254.

[31]Ibid., 252.

[32]Ibid., 402.

[33]Morrill, 4.

[34]George F. Scheer and Hugh F. Rankin, *Rebels and Redcoats: The American Revolution Through the Eyes of Those Who Fought and Lived It* (Cambridge: Da Capo Press, 1987), 132.

[35]Mackesy, 213.

[36]Hibbert, 104.

[37]Ibid., 248-249.

[38]Ibid., 249.

[39]Mackesy, 403.

[40]Ibid., 404.

[41]Ibid.

[42]Hibbert, 269.

[43]Ibid.

[44]John Buchanan, *The Road to Guilford Courthouse: The American Revolution in the Carolinas* (New York: John Wiley & Sons, Inc., 1997), 94.

[45]Walter B. Edgar, *Partisans and Redcoats: The Southern Conflict that Turned the Tide of the American Revolution* (New York: HarperCollins, 2003), 64.

[46]Ibid.

[47]Melvin B. Endy Jr., "Just War, Holy War, and Millennialism in Revolutionary America," *William and Mary Quarterly* 42, no. 1 (January 1985): 18.

[48]Ibid., 9.

[49]Edgar, 54.

[50]Morrill, 96.

[51]Ibid., 68.

CHAPTER 3

SELF-DEFEATING POLICIES

The second factor that contributed to the failure British strategy in the south in

1780 and 1781 was the application of self-defeating political and military policies. This

chapter explores General Clinton's failure to reestablish civilian government following

his capture of Charleston. It also analyzes his decision to withdraw his support for

neutrality among the southern populace. Following that, it examines the failure of British

commanders to convince local leaders to join the loyalist cause. Next, it focuses on

British and loyalist atrocities against rebels and civilians. Lastly, it analyzes British

policy on slavery and Indians. British commanders in the south undermined Lord

Germain's strategy of rallying public support through self-defeating political and military

policy. This led directly to the strategy's failure.

Following General Clinton's capture of Charleston in May 1780, his way seemed

clear to implement Lord Germain's strategy and rally local support for British rule.

Germain's first directive to Clinton was to establish a southern peace commission.

Germain's goal was to reestablish civilian government, end the rule of British military

law, and foster a working relationship between British commanders and local leaders.

Germain believed that this would allow Clinton and Cornwallis to recruit loyalist militias

to bring about the final defeat of the rebellion. However, Germain's lofty goals for the

peace commission were never fulfilled. This was due primarily to a serious personality

conflict between the members of the commission.

A few days after Clinton captured Charleston, he learned that he was no longer to

be the sole member of the peace commission. Germain directed him to share power with

Admiral Marriot Arbuthnot, commander of all British naval forces in North America. Although Clinton and Arbuthnot had worked closely together during the siege of Charleston, Clinton detested Arbuthnot. Arbuthnot was a former dockyard commissioner and in poor health. First Lord of the Admiralty Sandwich promoted him to his position as naval commander in chief. Lord Charles Laughton described Arbuthnot's promotion as "a sample of the extremity to which the maladministration of Lord Sandwich had reduced the navy" and described Arbuthnot as "a late survival . . . ignorant of the discipline of his profession . . . destitute of even a rudimentary knowledge of naval tactics . . . a coarse, blustering, foul-mouthed bully."[1]

Germain included Arbuthnot on the peace commission due to Sandwich's influence within Lord North's Ministry. Clinton felt that Germain had slighted his authority as commander in chief with this decision. He threatened to resign unless Germain gave him a veto on the reestablishment of civilian government. Clinton wrote that Arbuthnot was "FALSE AS HELL. He swore that he would act with me . . . and if he ever did otherwise or deceived me, he hoped he would be damned. The gentleman swears most horribly and I believe will LIE – NAY, I KNOW HE WILL IN A THOUSAND INSTANCES."[2]

Arbuthnot sided with Germain. The admiral was eager to use the commission's power to reestablish civilian government in the south. Clinton disagreed and used his influence to maintain military control. Arbuthnot became discouraged by this turn of events and wrote, "At present we seem to be so wedded to our military power that it will not be parted with until it cannot be avoided."[3]

Arbuthnot insisted on publishing the terms of a future political settlement in the south. He sent a letter to Germain requesting that he order Clinton to comply. This deepened the antagonism between Arbuthnot and Clinton and led to the breakdown of the peace commission. In the end, the only point on which Clinton and Arbuthnot agreed was to grant clemency to rebels who turned themselves in to British authority.[4] This was the sole accomplishment of Germain's southern peace commission in 1780.

It is not clear whether Clinton blocked Germain's goal of reestablishing civil government in the south simply because Arbuthnot agreed with it, or because he was opposed to it on principle. Unfortunately for Germain, Clinton's efforts made it more difficult for Cornwallis to rally southern support than if a local loyalist government had been in place. Such a government would have assisted the British by counterbalancing the influence of the patriot committees of safety that operated throughout the region.

Clinton's decision to withdraw his support for neutrality among the southern populace was another self-defeating British policy. On 3 June 1780, Clinton issued a proclamation stating that former rebels who had accepted parole and withdrawn from the conflict were no longer allowed to remain neutral. This angered many of the local people because it replaced a more lenient policy that Clinton had announced after he captured Charleston. The previous policy granted parolees the privilege of remaining neutral; this one demanded that they swear allegiance to the king and actively support the British government. If a parolee refused to take the loyalty oath, Clinton would label him an enemy and have him arrested. Additionally, Clinton gave the former rebels only 17 days to decide whether or not to take the oath. Clinton wrote that this new policy was a "prudent measure" because under the earlier conditions a "great number of inveterate

31

rebels might remain in the country, and by their underhanded and secret counsel and

other machinations prevent the return of many well disposed persons to their

allegiance."[5]

This policy was seriously flawed. Most southerners felt no obligation to honor

their oath because Clinton forced them to swear allegiance under duress.[6] When

Cornwallis assumed command of all British forces in the south the following month, he

also rejected the past neutrality of the locals. He wrote, "In a civil war, there is no

admitting of neutral characters, & those who are not clearly with us must be so far

considered against us, as to be disarmed, and every measure taken to prevent their being

able to do mischief."[7] Clinton later admitted that this policy was counterproductive to the

British war effort. However, in his memoirs he sought to excuse himself from blame. He

wrote that since he departed South Carolina for New York less than a week after issuing

the proclamation, Cornwallis was responsible for the consequences because he had the

authority to overrule it.[8]

Clinton's neutrality policy also created a false impression of the number of

loyalists that existed in the south. A British officer named Captain Bowater recognized

that this policy was dangerous. He wrote to Lord Denbigh of the new loyalists, "I should

be very sorry to trust any of them out of my sight. They swallow the Oaths of Allegiance

to the King and Congress alternately with as much ease as your Lordship does poached

Eggs."[9]

Another failed initiative was the British attempt to convince local leaders to join

the loyalist cause. One example is Cornwallis's meeting with 76-year-old Richard

Richardson. Richardson was one of the most respected local leaders in South Carolina in the summer of 1780. Cornwallis offered him "any office or title he might wish" if he agreed to join the British cause. He also threatened to imprison Richardson if he did not accept the offer. Richardson replied, "I have from the best convictions of my mind embarked on a cause which I think righteous and just; I have knowingly staked my life, family, and property all upon the issue. I am prepared to suffer or triumph with it, and would rather die a thousand deaths than betray my country or deceive my friends."[10] Cornwallis imprisoned Richardson and the man died under confinement in September 1780.

British commanders also routinely treated local leaders with contempt and rarely attempted to win their support through compromise. Rather than employing these influential leaders for political gain, British commanders often subjected them to abuse. One example is the British treatment of Thomas Farr, speaker of the South Carolina House of Representatives. During Clinton's siege of Charleston, British troops captured Farr and his son. As they marched, a British commander forced Farr and his son to herd cattle in their supply train and held them up for public ridicule.[11]

The most counterproductive British behavior in the south was the numerous atrocities they committed against rebels and civilians. Stories of these crimes quickly spread throughout the backcountry and had an explosive effect on the populace. Although rebel leaders regularly exaggerated the stories for effect, the theme was consistent. Patriots used this propaganda to portray the British as unjust oppressors. They also portrayed loyalists as traitors living in their midst. Far from terrorizing the populace into submission, these atrocities only strengthened the patriot resistance and propaganda campaign.

In June 1780, Clinton established a series of fortified garrisons in the backcountry. They stretched from Georgetown on the South Carolina coast; northwest to Cheraw on the Pee Dee River; southwest to Camden, Hanging Rock, and Rocky Mount on the Catawba-Wateree River; west to Ninety-six near the Saluda River; and finally south to Augusta on the Savannah River (see figure 1). Clinton built these forts to provide safe refuge for loyalists in the backcountry and to serve as bases for British and loyalist troops. He realized that British control of the coastal cities of Wilmington, Charleston, and Savannah would not be enough to defeat the southern rebellion. By extending his reach into the backcountry, Clinton demonstrated his intent to fight the patriots in their home territory.

In August 1780, Cornwallis wrote a letter to the commander of the British garrison at Ninety-six, Lieutenant Colonel John Cruger. He ordered Cruger to punish "with the greatest rigour" any local citizen who had taken the loyalty oath and then participated in violence against British forces. Cornwallis directed him to imprison these people, seize their property, and compensate injured loyalists with the goods. He wrote that any "militia man who had borne arms with us and had afterwards joined the enemy should be immediately hanged." Cornwallis concluded by directing Cruger to "take the most vigorous measures to extinguish the rebellion in the district you command, and that you will obey in the strictest manner the directions I have given in this letter."[12]

During the war in the south, British officers became extremely frustrated at the rapid changing of sides by local militias. Cornwallis took the extreme measure of decreeing "instant death" on patriot prisoners of war who had switched sides and been captured following the Battle of Camden. British Lieutenant Colonel Charles Stedman

34

wrote that hanging captured rebels became "necessary to restrain their perfidy by examples of severity, and the terrors of punishment." Cornwallis personally witnessed the execution of these soldiers.[13] This encouraged Cornwallis's subordinates to follow his harsh example.

Although Cornwallis and his subordinates routinely executed rebel prisoners, the general expressed outrage after receiving reports of patriot militia abusing loyalist prisoners. In response, he vowed to "retaliate on the unfortunate persons" in his custody.[14] He also foreshadowed the eventual collapse of Germain's strategy by expressing little concern for the safety of southern loyalists who looked to him for protection. After rebels attacked a backcountry loyalist village in 1780, Cornwallis wrote, "When I see a whole settlement running away from 20 or 30 robbers, I think they deserve to be robbed."[15]

Cornwallis was not alone in his harsh methods. Lieutenant Colonel Banastre Tarleton was his most infamous subordinate commander. Tarleton personified the British reputation for brutality towards the southern populace in 1780 and 1781. He was born in Liverpool to a wealthy family in 1754. Tarleton's father was mayor of the city and purchased a commission for his son in the King's Dragoon Guards in 1775. Tarleton's contemporaries described him as "almost femininely beautiful," extremely vain, argumentative, and unscrupulous. Horace Walpole reported that Tarleton boasted "of having butchered more men and lain with more women than anyone else in the Army," although historians generally believe that raped is a more accurate description than lain.[16]

Tarleton commanded the British Legion. This was a unit of dragoons that was almost entirely made up of American loyalists. In 1778, the British Army formed the

Legion in New York by combining a number of formerly independent units including the Philadelphia Light Dragoons, the Caledonian Volunteers, and Kinloch's Light Dragoons. Tarleton's Legion performed scouting and raiding duties and occasionally fought as dismounted infantry in the British battle line.

On 29 May 1780, Tarleton made his reputation at the Battle of Waxhaws. This engagement became more widely known in the south as Buford's Massacre. From that point on, southerners widely referred to Tarleton as "Bloody Tarleton." On that day, Colonel Abraham Buford and his 400 Virginia Continentals were marching through the Waxhaws District of central South Carolina. The Continental Army had sent them south to reinforce Lincoln's southern patriot army at Charleston earlier that month. When Buford learned of Lincoln's surrender, he turned the unit around and headed north. At that time, Buford's small force was the largest unit of regular patriot troops left in the south.

Buford believed that there were no enemy troops in the area and was marching at a leisurely pace. At approximately 3:00 P.M., his scouts heard bugles and horses nearby. Cornwallis had dispatched Tarleton and 270 of his British Legion from the coast to track down and destroy Buford. They had covered 150 miles in 54 hours on horseback and caught up with Buford--a remarkable achievement.

Uncharacteristically, Tarleton initially offered Buford the chance to surrender. Buford replied, "I reject your proposals, and shall defend myself to the last extremity."[17] However, he made a crucial error and ordered his men to hold their fire until Tarleton's dragoons were only ten yards away. Buford's volley did not slow the loyalists. Tarleton's men rode into the patriots and began a one-sided massacre.[18] According to eyewitness accounts, the loyalists kept up the slaughter even after Buford raised a white flag and asked for quarter. A patriot surgeon named Robert Brownfield accompanied Buford and wrote, "The demand for quarter, seldom refused to a vanquished foe, was at once found to be in vain."[19] Other witnesses reported that Tarleton's troops tossed aside patriot corpses to stab and club the wounded lying underneath. Tarleton later wrote that his troops fought with a "vindictive asperity not easily restrained." However, he wrote in his memoirs that their behavior was initiated by their mistaken belief that "they had lost their commanding officer."[20]

The results of the battle were terrible for the patriots. Buford lost 113 killed and 150 wounded while Tarleton had only five killed and 14 wounded. Following the battle, local women from the Waxhaw Presbyterian Church brought wagons to carry off the wounded and dug trenches to bury the mutilated patriots. They buried 84 bodies in one mass grave and 25 in another.[21] Doctor Brownfield wrote a graphic description of the loyalists' attack on a patriot officer:

> Early in the sanguinary conflict he was attacked by a dragoon, who aimed many deadly blows at his head, all of which by the dextrous use of the small sword he easily parried; when another on the right, by one stroke, cut off his right hand through the metacarpal bones. He was then assailed by both, and instinctively attempted to defend his head with his left arm until the forefinger was cut off, and the arm hacked in eight or ten places from the wrist to the shoulder. His head was then laid open almost the whole length of the crown to the eye brows.[22]

Brownfield also described the dragoons' attack on another of Buford's wounded officers:

> In a short time Tarleton's bugle was heard, and a furious attack was made on the rear guard, commanded by Lieut. Pearson. Not a man escaped. Poor Pearson was inhumanely mangled on the face as he lay on his back. His nose and lip were bisected obliquely; several of his teeth were broken out in the upper jaw, and the under completely divided on each side. These wounds were inflicted after he had fallen, with several others on his head, shoulders and arms.[23]

News of this battle traveled quickly throughout the south and the name Bloody Tarleton became well known to the local populace. Local leaders and clergy seized on the story of Buford's Massacre to rally southerners to the patriot cause. A phrase that came to prominence because of this battle was "Tarleton's Quarter," which meant give no quarter and take no prisoners. Patriot militia used this phrase to justify extreme measures when battling loyalists or British troops. Patriot propagandists also used this slogan as a tool to inflame the local populace and remind them of British tyranny.

Events that occurred at a June 1780 community meeting in the Waxhaws district were typical of the explosive effect of Buford's Massacre. Cornwallis sent a loyalist politician to threaten the Waxhaws residents with severe consequences if they did not abandon the patriot cause. The representative read a proclamation asserting that the British had defeated Washington's army, the Continental Congress had abandoned the south, and the patriot cause was dead. Before he could finish his speech, community leader William Hill stood up and challenged the man. Hill reminded his neighbors, "We has all taken an oath to defend & maintain the Independence of the state to the utmost of our power, we had an open side, we could keep in a body, go into North Carolina meet our friends & return with them to recover our state."[24]

The crowd's reaction to Hill's speech was electric. They cheered him and Hill reported that the loyalist was "obliged to disappear with his proclamation and protections for fear of the resentment of the audience."[25] Hill convinced his neighbors to form a new patriot militia regiment and they elected him as one of its colonels. Word spread quickly about the new unit and men from South Carolina and Georgia came forward to join up. Communities throughout the backcountry raised similar militias as reports of Buford's

Massacre continued to spread. Although other southern militia leaders such as Thomas Sumter and Francis Marion attained greater fame, William Hill was the first local leader in the backcountry to rally the people to the rebellion following Lincoln's surrender at Charleston.

Tarleton was not alone among Cornwallis's subordinates in provoking intense southern anger. Major James Wemyss was a British officer who worked throughout 1780 to recruit southern loyalists along South Carolina's northern border. His goal was to form a unit of South Carolina rangers to oppose the local patriot militias. Wemyss recruited a local man named John Harrison to command the unit. He commissioned Harrison as a militia major and appointed his two brothers, Robert and Samuel, as captains. Wemyss wanted Harrison to recruit 500 loyalists for the unit. However, Harrison was never able to attract more than 100. Like Tarleton's Legion, Wemyss's South Carolina Rangers were almost exclusively American loyalists.

Like Cornwallis and Tarleton, Wemyss did not seem to grasp the self-defeating nature of the abuse his men inflicted on their neighbors. He sometimes referred to his rangers as "banditti" and "plunderers." Their behavior outraged the local people and patriot militias soon targeted Harrison and his brothers for assassination. Rebels killed Robert in battle and shot John and Samuel while they slept in their beds. All three men were dead by the end of 1780.[26]

Wemyss allowed his troops to plunder local farms, burn houses, confiscate personal property, execute prisoners, and menace civilians. He declared his hatred for the Presbyterian religion of many of the local Scotch-Irish immigrants and burned a number of backcountry Presbyterian churches. Wemyss referred to these places of worship as "sedition shops."[27] This brutal treatment shocked even local loyalists. A community leader named Francis Kinloch recognized the self-defeating nature of these tactics. He wrote to a British official that Wemyss's treatment of civilians "would make you and every worthy Englishman blush for the degeneracy of the Nation."[28]

These atrocities were instrumental in sparking the bitter civil war between southern loyalists and patriots throughout the backcountry in the summer of 1780. Both sides were guilty of cruel behavior towards their neighbors in this conflict. This cycle of brutality and retribution became one of the defining characteristics of the war in the south. A Swedish officer serving with the French navy named Karl Gustav Tornquist described a typical scene that occurred that summer: "On a beautiful estate a pregnant woman was found murdered in her bed through several bayonet stabs. The barbarians had opened both of her breasts and written above the bed canopy, 'Thou shalt never give birth to a rebel.'" In the next room, the loyalist militia arranged five decapitated patriot heads in a cupboard.[29]

During that summer, patriot militias proved to be equally as severe in their methods. They often invoked the well known name of Bloody Tarleton and his treatment of Buford's troops to justify their behavior. A patriot militiaman from Rowan County, North Carolina named Moses Hall described a "scene that made a lasting impression" on his conscience:

> I was invited by some of my comrades to go and see some of the prisoners. We went to where six were standing together. Some discussion taking place, I heard some of our men cry out, "Remember Buford," and the prisoners were immediately hewed to pieces with broadswords. At first I bore the scene without any emotion, but upon a moment's reflection, I felt such horror as I never did before nor have since, and, returning to my quarters and throwing myself upon my blanket, I contemplated the cruelties of war until overcome and unmanned by

a distressing gloom from which I was not relieved until commencing our march next morning before day by moonlight.[30]

Roving bands that followed the regular forces and militias throughout the south also contributed to the bitter nature of the conflict. Many of these gangs were made up of men and women who robbed their neighbors of their valuables. A loyalist officer recorded this description:

> The outrages were mostly committed by a train of loyal refugees, as they termed themselves, whose business it was to follow the camps and under the protection of the army enrich themselves on the plunder they took from the distressed inhabitants who were not able to defend it.
>   We were also distressed by another form of beings (not better than harpies). These were women who followed the army in the character of soldiers' and officers' wives. They were generally considered by the inhabitants to be more insolent than the soldiers. They were generally mounted on the best horses and side saddles, dressed in the finest and best clothes that could be taken from the inhabitants as the army marched through the country.[31]

British and loyalist women were not the only ladies who played a key role in this conflict. In some southern families it was the wife who convinced her husband to join the rebellion. In South Carolina, Isabella Ferguson had a bitter dispute with her brother-in-law, loyalist Colonel James Ferguson. After he attempted to recruit her husband, she responded, "I am a rebel, my brothers are rebels, and the dog Trip is a rebel, too." She reminded her husband of Tarleton and Wemyss's treatment of their neighbors and warned him, "Now, in the presence of the British army, if you go with them you may stay with them, for I can no longer be your wife." He did not join the loyalists.[32]

Although Cornwallis did not anticipate that the war in the south would descend to these levels, he inadvertently set the events in motion by his own policies. He ordered and carried out the summary executions of local patriots who violated their loyalty oaths. He also permitted Tarleton, Wemyss, and others to execute prisoners and burn rebel property. Even though Cornwallis wrote that he would "severely punish any act of cruelty," cruel British behavior was common in the south in 1780 and 1781.[33]

Inevitably, news of these atrocities reached London. When Lord Germain heard the reports he was outraged. He believed that British abuses would spell disaster for his strategy of rallying local support in the south. As events later demonstrated, he proved to be correct. Germain wrote to Cornwallis and demanded that he impose discipline on his troops, "The great mischief Complain'd of in the prosecution of the war is that relaxation of discipline which disgraces the army and has alienated the Affections of the inhabitants from the Royal Cause."[34] Germain recognized the self-defeating nature of this behavior and attempted to impose his will on his commanders from across the Atlantic. He wrote to Clinton in New York, "Our utmost efforts will fail of their effects if we cannot find the means to engage the people of America in support of a cause which is equally their own and ours . . . induce them to employ their own force to protect themselves in the enjoyment of the blessings of the [British] constitution to which they shall have been restored."[35]

British policy on slavery and Indians also undermined Germain's strategy. By the summer of 1780, British officials in America had already established a long tradition of opposition to the southern slave trade. Former Royal Governor of Virginia Lord Dunmore suggested that slaves who rebelled against patriot masters and declared their loyalty to the king might win their freedom. In a statement to patriots threatening to seize an ammunition store he wrote, "By the living God, if an insult is offered to me or those who have obeyed my orders, I will declare freedom to the slaves and lay the town in ashes."[36]

Months later Dunmore made good on his promise and issued an emancipation proclamation while safely aboard a British warship. He wrote, "I do hereby further declare all indented servants, Negroes or others, (appertaining to Rebels) free, that are able and willing to bear arms, they joining his Majesty's Troops as soon as may be, for the more speedily reducing this Colony to a proper sense of duty to His Majesty's crown and dignity." [37] A southern journalist wrote in response, "Hell itself could not have vomitted anything more black than this design of emancipating our slaves."[38]

The first black indentured servants arrived at Jamestown, Virginia in 1619. By 1700, most large southern plantation owners relied primarily on slaves to provide their labor. By 1775, slaves outnumbered whites in some southern states. South Carolina had 110,000 slaves and 90,000 whites. Georgia had 18,000 slaves and 10,000 whites. North Carolina had 20,000 slaves and 70,000 whites. North Carolina maintained a smaller proportion of slaves to whites than the other two states because it lacked the deep-water ports crucial to the plantation economy.[39]

Many southerners lived in constant fear of widespread slave rebellion. Local lady Janet Schaw reported a persistent rumor that British commanders had promised "every Negro that would murder his Master and family that he should have his Master's plantation."[40] Although there was little truth to this, the Wilmington Committee of Safety dispatched patrols to search for escaped slaves, disarm them, and return them to their owners.[41] Former South Carolina Royal Governor William Bull wrote about the rumor's effect: "Words, I am told, cannot express the flame that this occasioned amongst all ranks and degrees; the cruelty and savage barbarity of the scheme was the conversation of all companies."[42]

Southern revulsion to Lord Dunmore's emancipation proclamation set the tone for this aspect of the war. Cornwallis perpetuated this destructive policy in 1780 and 1781 by recruiting escaped slaves and employing them as loyalist troops. A rebel soldier named William Dobein James wrote a detailed description of a company of black dragoons in the south. Cornwallis formed this unit from escaped slaves who rallied near Charleston after Lincoln surrendered his patriot army in May 1780.[43] Cornwallis's decision to use escaped slaves as loyalist soldiers handed the southern rebels an important propaganda victory. It provided one more opportunity for them to hold up British officials as convenient hate symbols to the southern populace. The political damage that this policy caused Great Britain outweighed any military advantage that it provided.

British policy on Indians in the south also undermined Lord Germain's strategy. Since the end of the French and Indian War in 1763, British law allowed no white settlements west of the Appalachian Mountains. Throughout the 1760s and 1770s, bands of southern frontier families violated this policy and traveled westward. Many of them settled in the Tennessee and Virginia valleys of the Watauga, Holston, and Nolichucky Rivers. Southerners referred to these people as "Wataugans" or "over-mountain men." These settlers were opportunists who cleared plots of land in the forest, built cabins, raised crops, and grazed farm animals on land the British insisted still belonged to the local Cherokee Indians.

Although the Cherokee were keenly aware of the settlers' appetite for land, they were also enamored of the supplies the Wataugans brought for trade. These included rum, firearms, ammunition, and manufactured goods. In 1772 the Cherokee agreed to lease land to the settlers for ten years. In 1775, they signed a treaty with a North Carolina businessman named Richard Henderson and sold him huge tracts of land in the region. When hostilities erupted between the British and the Americans later that year, the Cherokee were caught in a difficult dilemma. They were forced to choose between their British allies and their American business partners.

In April 1776, British Superintendent for the Southern Indian Department John Stuart dispatched his brother to the village of Chota on the Little Tennessee River.[44] Henry Stuart's goal was to convince the Cherokee to declare their allegiance to Great Britain rather than the American rebels. Although the patriots also pursued an alliance with the Cherokee, the Indians ultimately sided with the British. A Cherokee war chief named Dragging Canoe believed the British offered the greatest protection for their tribal territory. Stuart issued a proclamation that demanded all Wataugans vacate their farms and move east of the Appalachian Mountains within 20 days. The Wataugans ignored the proclamation and prepared for war with the Cherokee and the British.

In July 1776, the southern backcountry exploded as Dragging Canoe led hundreds of Cherokee warriors on raids against Wataugan villages. This was the beginning of what came to be known as the Cherokee War. On 14 July 1776, patriot General Griffith Rutherford reported, "The Indins is making Grate Prograce, in Distroying and Murdering, in the frunteers of the County."[45] The following month, Rutherford led 2,500 North Carolina militia and 1,800 South Carolina militia through the Blue Ridge Mountains and into Cherokee territory. They burned a number of Cherokee villages and destroyed their cornfields. This deprived many Indians of their shelter and food stores. In October, patriot Colonel William Christian led another expedition and destroyed more Cherokee settlements.[46]

The Cherokee never recovered. Additionally, their alliance with Great Britain served as an important patriot propaganda tool for years to follow. Rebel leaders pointed to the alliance and the Cherokee violence as yet another example of British tyranny. When Henry Stuart attempted to negotiate a peace treaty between the Cherokee and the Wataugans, rebel leaders successfully spread the rumor that he had incited the Cherokee attack. This widely held belief undermined British legitimacy in the south and contributed to the failure of Germain's strategy.

The British also used Indians as loyalist troops. During General Andrew Pickens's attack on Fort Cornwallis near Augusta in May 1781, British Lieutenant Colonel Thomas Browne employed 300 Creek Indians as defenders. Browne surrendered in early June and the rebels captured hundreds of his men.[47] As the British evacuated Augusta and Savannah, the Cherokee and Chickasaw sought a peace treaty with the Americans. However, the Creek continued to side with the British and serve as loyalist militia.[48] Throughout 1780 and 1781, this alliance provided important propaganda material to the patriots. By appealing to widespread backcountry fear of renewed Indian attacks, rebel leaders rallied more southerners to their cause. Any military advantage that Cornwallis may have gained from using Indians as loyalist troops was outweighed by the political damage that this policy caused.

Although Cornwallis did not agree with Germain's strategy, it is unlikely that he deliberately set out to undermine it. Nevertheless, this was the effect of many of his policies. Cornwallis was an aggressive, ambitious officer who focused on pursuing traditional battle with the southern patriots. He never believed in Germain's strategy of rallying public support to defeat the rebellion. It was simply not in keeping with his training or experience as an 18th-century British Army officer.

Prior to his departure for New York in June 1780, Clinton authorized Cornwallis to conduct offensive operations as long as they did not jeopardize the loss of southern territory. Cornwallis violated that guidance and abandoned Germain's strategy. Clinton wrote in his memoirs that Cornwallis "withdrew from South Carolina . . . in direct disobedience of the orders left with him by his Commander in Chief." He concluded, "I fear we can only lament so destructive a misapplication of his talents . . . to ascribe the smallest military merit to such conduct."[49]

Clearly, British commanders employed a number of self-defeating political and military policies while attempting to defeat the southern rebellion. Clinton opposed the reestablishment of civil government in the south and forced the people to choose sides by demanding loyalty oaths. Similarly, Cornwallis failed to engage local leaders, executed prisoners, and permitted his subordinates to abuse the populace. Both commanders also provoked southern anger by employing slaves and Indians as loyalist militia. These self-defeating policies undermined Lord Germain's strategy by provoking widespread southern anger and sustaining the rebel propaganda effort in 1780 and 1781. This led directly to the strategy's failure.

Chapter 4 examines the British failure to deploy sufficient forces to control the south and protect southern loyalists. It explores the reasons behind Great Britain's attempt to accomplish this difficult task with a 4,000-man army. Next, it surveys patriot militia victories against British and loyalist forces throughout the southern backcountry.

Lastly, it analyzes the patriot destruction of loyalist forces led by Major Patrick Ferguson

at the Battle of King's Mountain on 7 October 1780.

[1] Piers Mackesy, *The War for America, 1775-1783* (Lincoln, Nebraska: University of Nebraska Press, 1993), 341.

[2] Christopher Hibbert, *Redcoats and Rebels: The American Revolution Through British Eyes* (New York: W. W. Norton & Company, 2002), 268.

[3] Mackesy, 342.

[4] Ibid.

[5] William B. Willcox, ed., *The American Rebellion: Sir Henry Clinton's Narrative of His Campaigns, 1775-1782, with an Appendix of Original Documents* (New Haven: Yale University Press, 1954), 181.

[6] Don Higginbotham, *The War of American Independence: Military Attitudes, Policies, and Practice, 1763-1789* (Boston: Northeastern University Press, 1983), 360.

[7] Walter B. Edgar, *Partisans and Redcoats: The Southern Conflict that Turned the Tide of the American Revolution* (New York: HarperCollins, 2003), 123-124.

[8] Willcox, *The American Rebellion*, 181.

[9] Hibbert, 268.

[10] Edgar, 128.

[11] Ibid., 50.

[12] Franklin and Mary Wickwire, *Cornwallis: The American Adventure* (Boston: Houghton Mifflin Company, 1970), 179.

[13] Robert S. Lambert, *South Carolina Loyalists in the American Revolution* (Columbia, South Carolina: University of South Carolina Press, 1987), 189.

[14] Edgar, 131.

[15] Mackesy, 344.

[16] Hibbert, 264.

[17] Dan L. Morrill, *Southern Campaigns of the American Revolution* (Baltimore: The Nautical & Aviation Publishing Company of America, 1993), 78.

[18]J. Tracy Power, "The Virtue of Humanity Was Totally Forgot: Buford's Massacre, May 29, 1780," *South Carolina Historical Magazine* 93, no. 1 (January 1992): 8.

[19]George F. Scheer and Hugh F. Rankin, *Rebels and Redcoats: The American Revolution Through the Eyes of Those Who Fought and Lived It* (New York: Da Capo Press, 1987), 402.

[20]Henry Steele Commager and Richard B. Morris, eds., *The Spirit of Seventy Six: The Story of the American Revolution as Told by Participants* (New York: Da Capo Press, 1995), 1115.

[21]Morrill, 79.

[22]Commager and Morris, 1112.

[23]Ibid., 1111.

[24]Edgar, 57.

[25]Ibid., 58.

[26]Ibid., 60.

[27]Ibid., 62.

[28]Jerome J. Nadelhaft, *Disorders of War: The Revolution in South Carolina* (Orono, Maine: University of Maine Press, 1982), 58.

[29]Hibbert, 273.

[30]Ibid.

[31]Ibid., 274.

[32]Edgar, 63.

[33]Ibid., 61.

[34]Stephen Conway, "'The great mischief Complain'd of': Reflections on the Misconduct of British Soldiers in the Revolutionary War," *William and Mary Quarterly* 47, no. 3 (July 1990): 370.

[35]R. Arthur Bowler, *Logistics and the Failure of the British Army in America, 1775-1783* (Princeton: Princeton University Press, 1975), 50.

[36]Morrill, 31.

[37]Benjamin Quarles, *The Negro in the American Revolution* (Chapel Hill: University of North Carolina Press, 1961), 19.

[38]Ibid., 20.

[39]Morrill, 31-32.

[40]Ibid., 32.

[41]Ibid.

[42]Ibid., 33.

[43]Henry Lumpkin, *From Savannah to Yorktown: The American Revolution in the South* (Lincoln, Nebraska: toExcel Press, 2000), 51.

[44]Morrill, 29.

[45]Ibid., 30.

[46]Ibid., 31.

[47]John S. Pancake, *This Destructive War: The British Campaign in the Carolinas, 1780-1782* (Tuscaloosa: University of Alabama Press, 1985), 202.

[48]James H. O' Donnell III, *Southern Indians in the American Revolution* (Knoxville: University of Tennessee Press, 1972), 125-129.

[49]Willcox, *The American Rebellion*, 271.

CHAPTER 4

INSUFFICIENT FORCES

The third factor that led to the failure of Lord Germain's strategy was the British

failure to deploy sufficient forces to control the south and protect southern loyalists. This

chapter explores the reasons behind the British government's attempt to accomplish this

difficult task with a 4,000-man army. Next, it surveys patriot militia battlefield success

against British and loyalist forces throughout the backcountry during the second half of

1780. Lastly, it analyzes the patriot militia victory over loyalist forces led by Major

Patrick Ferguson at the Battle of King's Mountain on 7 October 1780.

By the time General Henry Clinton captured Charleston in May 1780, Great

Britain was involved in a global war that stretched its resources to the limits of its

capability. Following General Horatio Gates's spectacular victory against General John

Burgoyne's army at Saratoga, France formally recognized American independence. In

June 1778 France declared war on Great Britain. France's entry into the war changed the

nature of the conflict. The British were now forced to provide troops and supplies to

reinforce their plantations in India and guard their islands in the Caribbean. In North

America, Clinton desperately needed those troops and supplies to defeat the rebellion.

In April 1779, France and Spain concluded an alliance against Great Britain with

the Convention of Aranjuez. The Spanish planned to fight the British until they captured

Gibraltar. French goals were to recover Senegal and Dominica, capture Newfoundland,

reestablish presence in India, and acquire logging rights in Honduras.[1] On 16 August

1779, England was thrown into an invasion panic when a combined French and Spanish

fleet of 63 warships entered the English Channel and anchored off Plymouth. For the first time in 90 years, an enemy fleet was in possession of the English Channel. The French

also placed 31,000 troops at St. Malo and La Havre as an invasion force. George III

countered with 35 British warships, 21,000 regular troops, and 30,000 militia. British

Commander in Chief Lord Amherst deployed these forces to patrol the coast of Kent and

Sussex and placed a strategic reserve near London.[2] In September, the French fleet

returned to port to resupply and Spain recalled its fleet to prepare for an attack on

Gibraltar. Throughout 1779, British and French fleets also battled in the Caribbean, off

the coast of India, and in European waters.

Holland's entry into the war in 1780 also increased the strain on Great Britain's

resources. Holland was a member of the League of Armed Neutrality along with Russia,

Sweden, and Denmark. The Dutch wanted free access to French and Spanish ports that

the British had placed under blockade. Great Britain suspended Dutch commercial treaty

privileges in April 1780 and subjected their shipping to seizure. Although Holland's

allies in the League did not come to its aid, the Dutch had already opened negotiations

with Congress to form an alliance against Great Britain.[3]

Lord North now faced the dilemma of how best to divide his military resources

between numerous competing interests. Clinton continued fighting the rebels in America.

British fleets and garrisons defended against invasion at home. They also guarded against

French fleets in the Caribbean and along the North American coast. British troops

defended Gibraltar against Spanish attack and reinforced garrisons in India. Holland's

entry into the war gave France an important base at the Dutch island of Ceylon. The

Dutch also controlled the Cape of Good Hope which was the source of supply for the

French base at Mauritius. As a result, the British deployed 3,000 troops to capture the Cape of Good Hope and mobilized 2,000 troops to reinforce their bases in India.[4]

In 1780, Clinton's forces in America numbered 32,000. Approximately 27,000 of those were fit for duty. They included 1,862 in Nova Scotia, 14,285 in New York, 4,870 in South Carolina, 1,259 in Georgia, and 1,078 in Florida.[5] Clinton's only uncommitted reserve was in New York where he could field 5,000 troops to maneuver against Washington's northern army, if necessary. Clinton believed that he was undermanned and pressed Germain constantly for reinforcements during this period.

In late 1779, a report reached London indicating that French Admiral d'Estaing was sailing for the West Indies with a fleet of warships and 6,000 troops. The British Admiralty believed that d'Estaing was intent on capturing Jamaica. This caused an immediate response from businessmen in London who demanded the government reinforce the British garrisons in the Caribbean. The cabinet decided to take 5,000 of Clinton's troops to reinforce the West Indies against d'Estaing's invasion. Germain sent a letter to Clinton demanding that he provide the men. He knew this would enrage Clinton and attempted to soften the blow by writing, "Such a mark of attention to the security of the sugar colonies would give great pleasure to all ranks in this country."[6]

In response, Clinton submitted his resignation. He sent Duncan Drummond to London to present his grievances. When Drummond met with Germain, the secretary pretended astonishment at Clinton's resignation. Germain exclaimed, "Good God, Mr. Drummond! Is it possible that Sir Henry Clinton can think of desiring to come home at this critical time, when [the country] looks upon him as the only chance we have of saving America?"[7] Germain rejected Clinton's resignation and ordered Drummond back to New York.

During their meeting, Germain explained to Drummond the nature of Great Britain's global war with France and Spain. He convinced Drummond that British troops were more urgently needed in India and the Caribbean than in North America. Drummond wrote to Clinton, "Good God, my dear General, could you but know the situation this country is drove to! . . . How can a Minister send supplies when there are so few resources and so many demands? . . . If the force you require is not, cannot, be sent you to effect the service wished for, I think I can assure you no blame will fall to your share."[8]

Clinton fell into a dark depression when he learned that Germain refused to send him reinforcements. Lieutenant Colonel Charles Stuart reported that, "With tears in his eyes," Clinton told him that he was "quite an altered man," that his command now "oppressed him," and that he felt "incapable of his station." Clinton declared:

> Believe me, my dear Colonel Stuart. I envy even that grenadier who is passing the door, and would exchange with joy situations. No, let me advise you never to take command of an army. I know I am hated-nay, detested-in this army. But I am indifferent about it because I know it is without a cause. But I am determined to return home; the Minister has used me so ill that I can no longer bear with this life.[9]

Clinton's relationship with Admiral Arbuthnot also continued to deteriorate. Poor coordination prevented them from responding to French Admiral Chevalier de Ternay. He sailed six ships of the line to Newport, Rhode Island in August 1780. The French admiral established a base there with 4,000 troops and took control of what he called "the best and noblest harbour in America."[10] Washington added to Clinton's troubles by gathering his forces and threatening the British garrison at Staten Island.

With these threats in the north, Clinton was in no position to reinforce Cornwallis in the south. In fact, Clinton asked Cornwallis to send 2,500 of his own troops to him in New York to counter the French at Newport.[11] However, Clinton soon realized that Cornwallis did not have a man to spare.

Cornwallis's southern army numbered about 4,000 regular and loyalist troops. More than 3,000 of them were assigned to defend the British garrisons spread throughout the backcountry. Along the northern border of South Carolina, Cornwallis had 1,200 troops in four outposts: Hanging Rock, Rocky Mount, Cheraw, and Fairforest. He stationed another 1,500 at his remaining bases including Camden, Ninety-six, Georgetown, and Augusta (see figure 1).[12]

Cornwallis's army was made up of six British infantry regiments, two German infantry regiments, and six American loyalist regiments. The British infantry regiments were the Seventh, 23rd, 33rd, 63rd, 64th, and 71st. The two German regiments were the Huyne and the Ditfurth. The loyalist regiments were Tarleton's British Legion, the Volunteers of Ireland, the New York Volunteers, the Prince of Wales American Regiment, the South Carolina Royalists, and the North Carolina Volunteers.[13]

Cornwallis attempted to defeat the southern rebellion with these 4,000 troops. He would not receive any reinforcements from Germain or Clinton. This was primarily because the North Ministry viewed Cornwallis's campaign as a relatively minor effort in the larger global war with France, Spain, and Holland.

Cornwallis was responsible for defeating the rebellion in the southern states of North Carolina, South Carolina, and Georgia. North Carolina covers 52,000 square miles.

It contains three geographical regions: the Mountains, Piedmont, and Coastal Plain. In 1780, North Carolina contained about 276,000 people with 49,000 white males over 16.[14]

South Carolina spans 31,000 square miles. It also contains three regions: the Blue Ridge Mountains, Piedmont, and Coastal Plain. There were about 174,000 people with 24,000 white males over 16 in South Carolina in 1780.[15]

Georgia covers 58,000 square miles. It contains five regions: the Cumberland Plateau, Blue Ridge Mountains, Ridge and Valley Region, Piedmont Plateau, and Coastal Plain. The population in Georgia in 1780 was about 57,000 people with 9,000 white males over 16.[16]

As these figures indicate, Cornwallis was attempting to use 4,000 troops to establish control over a massive area and population. The territory consisted of 11 southern regions that spanned 141,000 square miles and contained about 507,000 people with 82,000 white males over 16. Germain and Clinton expected him to accomplish this with no reinforcements. This was clearly an enormously difficult task.

During the summer of 1780, backcountry patriots successfully exploited Cornwallis's weakness in numbers. Between 12 July and 7 October, southern rebels fought 22 engagements with British troops and loyalists. Of these 22 battles, 17 occurred in the backcountry.[17] One early example of these engagements occurred on 20 June 1780 at Ramsour's Mill, North Carolina.

Ramsour's Mill was about 20 miles north of South Carolina's northern border and 30 miles northwest of Charlotte. A loyalist officer named Lieutenant Colonel John Moore ordered local volunteers to gather supplies and prepare for Cornwallis's invasion of North Carolina. At that time, patriot General Griffith Rutherford was near Charlotte with 700 troops. He was tracking British forces in the Waxhaws District and ordered Colonel Francis Lock to attack Moore's loyalists. Major William Davie reported that Rutherford and Lock "agreed to attack Moores camp at Ramsours. . . . For this purpose Col Lock marched to cross the [Catawba] River at Sherrills & Beatie's fords while General Rutherford also moved to cross below."[18]

Rutherford and Lock attacked Moore's 1,000 loyalists with 400 rebels and the battle quickly deteriorated into hand-to-hand combat. Like many of the backcountry engagements, the Battle of Ramsour's Mill was characterized by vicious close combat and little control by officers. Captain Joseph Graham wrote, "After the actions commenced, scarcely any orders were given by the officers. They fought like common soldiers, and animated their men by their example, and they suffered severely. Captains Falls, Dobson, Smith, Bowman and Armstrong were killed; and Captains Houston and McKissick wounded."[19] Unofficial reports indicated that the rebels and loyalists each lost about an equal number, 140 killed and 200 wounded on each side.[20]

After the battle, Moore fled to the British base at Camden. The rebels had defeated him with a force less than half the size of his own. Cornwallis was furious with Moore for engaging the rebels prematurely. He realized that he was severely undermanned and that this patriot victory would encourage the rebel militias forming around him. He wrote, "The affair of Tryon County has given me great concern. Although I had my apprehensions that the flame would break out somewhere, the folly and imprudence of our friends are unpardonable."[21]

Another backcountry battle occurred three weeks later at James Williamson's plantation in South Carolina. The plantation was located 50 miles southwest of Charlotte,

North Carolina. Colonel George Turnbull was the commander of the British garrison at Rocky Mount, 50 miles southeast of Williamson's plantation. In July 1780, he wrote, "Some of the violent rebels . . . had returned to their plantations, and were encouraging the people to join them."[22] He ordered Captain Christian Huck to lead an expedition to "the frontier of the Province collecting all the royal militia with you in your march, and with said forces to push the rebels as far as you may deem convenient."[23]

Huck soon outraged the local people with his inflammatory rhetoric and cruel methods. Word spread that he was marching through the backcountry with 100 troops from Tarleton's Legion. Huck stunned the locals by declaring that even if they believed that "God almighty had become a Rebel, if there were 20 gods on that side, they would all be conquered." He vowed to track down and destroy all the local patriots even if they "were as thick as trees, and Jesus Christ himself were to command them." Word of this blasphemy soon spread throughout the region.[24]

At William Adair's home, Huck's troops threatened to hang Adair and stole his wife's shoe buckles and jewelry. In Reverend John Simpson's home, they vowed to scalp Simpson and present the scalp to his wife. In Martha Bratton's home, Huck's men placed a reaping hook at her neck. They vowed to cut off her head if she did not reveal the location of her husband, patriot Colonel William Bratton. At Mary McClure's home, Huck's men found molten pewter and bullet molds. Huck condemned her son and son-in-law as "violent rebels" and ordered them to be executed the next morning. When Mrs. McClure protested, one of Huck's men struck her with the flat of his sword.[25]

On 11 July 1780, Huck set up camp at James Williamson's plantation. His troops locked Mrs. McClure's son, son-in-law, and three other prisoners in a corncrib to await their execution. Colonel Bratton learned of Huck's assault on his wife that evening and rallied 250 of his neighbors to rescue the prisoners. Bratton and Captain John McClure caught Huck totally by surprise on the morning of 12 July at Williamson's plantation. The rebels withstood three loyalist bayonet charges and a patriot sharpshooter killed Huck with a shot to the head. After the battle, the rebels freed the prisoners from their corncrib jail unharmed.[26]

Patriot Colonel Richard Winn reported, "The enemies' loss, killed, wounded and prisoners, was considerable, besides, about one hundred horses, saddles, bridles, pistols, swords, and many other things." Rebel spy Joseph Kerr reported that Bratton's troops killed Huck and 98 of his men. Only 24 loyalists escaped. The rebels lost only one man killed and one wounded.[27]

The Battle of Williamson's Plantation became widely known in the south as Huck's Defeat. News of the rebel victory over Tarleton's Legion soon swelled General Thomas Sumter's local patriot militia to more than 600 troops. Patriot leaders used the victory as propaganda to illustrate British vulnerability. Patriot William Hill wrote that Huck's Defeat demonstrated that "the enemy were not invincible."[28]

The following month, Cornwallis inflicted a crushing defeat on the southern rebellion at the Battle of Camden. In July, Congress had selected General Horatio Gates to assume command of all American forces in the south. Prior to that, a Bavarian officer named Baron Johannes de Kalb was nominally in command. In April 1780, General George Washington had dispatched de Kalb from Morristown, New Jersey with 1,400 Maryland and Delaware Continentals. His mission was to assist General Benjamin Lincoln in the defense of Charleston. However, de Kalb did not even arrive in

Hillsborough until 22 June, more than a month after Lincoln had already surrendered. By that time, de Kalb's troops were the only regular patriot forces remaining south of the Potomac River.

Washington's choice to succeed de Kalb was General Nathanael Greene. Greene was a former Quaker from Rhode Island who possessed superb leadership and administrative skills. However, Congress overruled Washington and placed Gates in command. Greene described Gates as a "dirty little genius."[29]

On 16 August 1780, Gates unwisely decided to attack Lord Francis Rawdon's garrison at Camden, South Carolina. Gates had 3,052 troops. However, almost two-thirds of them were militia. Rawdon had 700 troops at Camden, but Cornwallis reinforced him with a large force on 13 August. This brought the total number of British troops at Camden to 2,043.[30] Cornwallis learned from a spy that Gates's army was almost totally made up of militia. On the night of 15 August, he decided to march his troops out of Camden and attack Gates at Rugeley's Mill. Before dawn on 16 August, Tarleton's British Legion engaged Colonel Charles Armand's dragoons and the two armies pulled back 500 yards to wait for daylight. At sunrise, Gates learned that he faced Cornwallis and his entire army, not just Rawdon's garrison. Colonel Otho Williams reported, "The general's astonishment could not be concealed."[31]

As was customary, Gates positioned his best troops on the right of his battle line. These were de Kalb's Maryland and Delaware Continentals. He placed his inexperienced Virginia and North Carolina militia in the center and on his left. Opposite Gates, Cornwallis also placed his best troops on his right. This meant that the veteran Royal Welsh Fusiliers, 23rd, and 33rd Regiments faced the most inexperienced American troops. Surprisingly, Gates ordered the Virginia militia to begin the battle and advance against the British regulars. They stood little chance. Cornwallis ordered a counterattack and the militia panicked. Many fled the battlefield without firing a shot. Gates watched as the British flanked the remainder of his army, destroyed his formations, and killed de Kalb.

It was a huge victory for Cornwallis. The Americans lost 800 killed and wounded and 1,000 captured. The British lost 88 killed and 245 wounded. Tarleton wrote, "After this last effort of continentals, rout and slaughter ensued in every quarter."[32] Gates had suffered a humiliating defeat and withdrew to Hillsborough, North Carolina with about 700 of his troops.

Cornwallis quickly became overconfident in victory. He falsely believed that he had defeated the rebellion in South Carolina and was free to move north. He wrote to Clinton, "I can leave South Carolina in security, and march with a great body of troops into the back part of North Carolina with the greatest probability of reducing that province to its duty."[33]

Cornwallis's optimism was misplaced. On 8 September 1780, he marched out of Camden with about 2,300 troops. He had begun his invasion of North Carolina and his initial objective was Charlotte. Once there, Cornwallis planned to resupply his army from local grist mills and continue on to Salisbury and Hillsborough. Although Cornwallis had defeated Gates, the British Army had also suffered. At Camden, the 33rd Regiment alone lost 36 percent of its soldiers and 50 percent of its officers.[34] This was a serious problem since Cornwallis could expect no reinforcements from Clinton or Germain. Every regular British soldier that Cornwallis lost in 1780 and 1781 was essentially irreplaceable.

Ominously, rebels had also begun attacking British supply wagons. The patriot militia struck as the convoys traveled between Cornwallis's coastal bases and his backcountry garrisons. Francis Marion led one of these units and his success rallied patriot sentiment throughout South Carolina. These successful raids suppressed the influence of the British victory at Camden. On 23 August, Cornwallis wrote to Clinton, "The Disaffection . . . of the Country East of the Santee is so great, that the Account of our Victory [at Camden] could not penetrate it--any person daring to speak of it being threatened with Death."[35]

The rebel attacks did not change Cornwallis's decision to invade North Carolina. He ordered Major Patrick Ferguson to march north with his seven loyalist battalions. Ferguson sent a letter to the backcountry rebels warning them to cease their attacks or he would "lay waste their country with fire and sword."[36] This threat only angered the rebels and they resolved to track down Ferguson and his troops. Patriot Colonel Isaac Shelby wrote, "It required no further taunt to rouse the patriotic indignation of Col. Shelby. He determined to make an effort to raise a force, in connection with other officers which should surprise and defeat Ferguson."[37] On 26 September, Shelby joined Colonels John Sevier, William Cleveland, and William Campbell. They rallied 900 local men and marched into the Blue Ridge Mountains in search of Ferguson and his loyalists.

On 30 September, Ferguson learned that the rebels were tracking him. He sent letters to Cornwallis in Charlotte and Lieutenant Colonel John Cruger at Ninety-six asking for reinforcements. He also alienated the local populace with his rhetoric. Ferguson told them, "If you choose to be pissed upon forever and ever by a set of mongrels, say so at once and let your women turn their backs upon you, and look out for real men to protect them."[38] Ferguson became worried when Cruger wrote that he could send no reinforcements because Ninety-six was also under threat of attack.

On 7 October 1780, Shelby, Sevier, Cleveland, Campbell and 1,300 of their rebels caught up with Ferguson and his 1,125 loyalists at King's Mountain on South Carolina's northern border. They took Ferguson and his men completely by surprise. The rebels advanced uphill towards the loyalists who returned fire ineffectively. Patriot James Collins reported, "The shot of the enemy soon began to pass over us like hail. Their great elevation above us had proved their ruin; they overshot us altogether."[39]

The rebels surrounded the loyalists. Ferguson attempted to form traditional battle lines, but the dense woods broke up his formations. The patriots made excellent use of their backcountry tactics and moved steadily forward. Rebel Thomas Young reported, "I stood behind one tree and fired until the bark was nearly all knocked off and my eyes pretty well filled with it."[40] Patriot Captain Alexander Chesney wrote that his troops "were able to advance to the crest . . . until they took post and opened an irregular but destructive fire from behind trees and other cover."[41] As the rebels reached the top, they shot Ferguson from his horse and massacred many of the remaining loyalists.

The patriots kept up the killing even after loyalist Captain Abraham DePeyster raised a white flag and asked for quarter. The rebels rallied each other with cries of "Tarleton's Quarter" and "Give them Buford's play!"[42] James Collins reported, "The dead lay in heaps on all sides, while the groans of the wounded were heard in every direction. I could not help turning away from the scene before me, with horror, and though exulting in victory, could not refrain from shedding tears."[43] In a final grotesque act, a group of patriots recalled Ferguson's warning to their neighbors that they would be "pissed upon forever." They seized Ferguson's corpse, stripped it, slashed it with a saber, and urinated on it.[44]

At King's Mountain, the loyalists lost 157 killed, 163 left to die, and 689 taken prisoner. The patriots lost 28 killed and 62 wounded. The rebel militia had inflicted a devastating setback to Cornwallis's invasion of North Carolina. It was also a serious blow to Germain's strategy of rallying local support for British rule. British Lieutenant Colonel Charles Stedman wrote, "Much had been expected from the exertions of Major Ferguson . . . and by his unfortunate fall and the slaughter, captivity or dispersion of his whole corps the plan of the expedition into North Carolina was entirely deranged."[45] Cornwallis agreed. He wrote that his loyalist militia near Ninety-six "was so totally disheartened by the defeat of Ferguson that of that whole district we could with difficulty assemble one hundred."[46]

After the battle, Clinton wrote, "No sooner had the news of it spread through the country than multitudes of disaffected flew to arms all parts, and menaced every British post on both frontiers, carrying terror even to the gates of Charleston."[47] The King's Mountain massacre was powerful motivation for southerners to avoid joining the loyalist cause. It also served as effective patriot propaganda. Local leaders spread stories of the wild animals that fed on the remains of the dead loyalists left to rot in the sun at King's Mountain. This sent an unmistakable warning to everyone in the region about the ultimate fate of southern loyalists. Clinton later wrote that the Battle of King's Mountain "unhappily proved the first link in a chain of evils that followed each other in regular succession until they at last ended in the total loss of America." [48]

With Great Britain involved in a global war in the summer of 1780, Germain and Clinton were unable to provide Cornwallis with enough troops to control the south and protect southern loyalists. Cornwallis inherited a series of backcountry garrisons when he assumed command from Clinton in June. He decided to use 75 percent of his 4,000 troops to protect these interior bases. This forced Cornwallis to maintain long lines of communication from the backcountry to his supply depots on the coast. Rebels successfully exploited this vulnerability by attacking British supply trains throughout the summer of 1780.

British commanders in the south found themselves surrounded by hostile communities. Although Cornwallis won an important victory at the Battle of Camden, it did not swing the southern populace in favor of British rule. The patriot massacre of Ferguson's loyalists at King's Mountain proved to be more effective in suppressing loyalist sentiment and rallying southerners to the rebellion.

Chapter 5 focuses on General Nathanael Greene's campaign against British forces in the south. It examines his use of mobile warfare against Cornwallis's army. Next, it explores Greene's effectiveness in rallying the support of local leaders. Following that, the chapter analyzes his use of patriot militias against British forces. Additionally, it examines Greene's battles with the British at Cowpens and Guilford Courthouse and Cornwallis's permanent withdrawal from the southern backcountry in April 1781. Lastly, the chapter surveys Greene's final battles to destroy British backcountry garrisons during the second half of 1781.

---

[1] Piers Mackesy, *The War for America, 1775-1783* (Lincoln, Nebraska: University of Nebraska Press, 1993), 262.

[2]Ibid., 290.

[3]Ibid., 378.

[4]Ibid., 380.

[5]Ibid., 346.

[6]Ibid., 309-310.

[7]Christopher Hibbert, *Redcoats and Rebels: The American Revolution Through British Eyes* (New York: W. W. Norton & Company, 2002), 249.

[8]Ibid., 250.

[9]Ibid.

[10]Mackesy, 349.

[11]Ibid., 346-347.

[12]Walter B. Edgar, *Partisans and Redcoats: The Southern Conflict that Turned the Tide of the American Revolution* (New York: HarperCollins, 2003), 88.

[13]Dan L. Morrill, *Southern Campaigns of the American Revolution* (Baltimore: The Nautical & Aviation Publishing Company of America, 1993), 89-90.

[14]William Thomas Sherman, *Calendar and Record of the Revolutionary War in the South: 1780-1781* (Seattle: William Thomas Sherman, 2003), 330.

[15]Ibid.

[16]Ibid.

[17]Don Higginbotham, *The War of American Independence: Military Attitudes, Policies, and Practice, 1763-1789* (Boston: Northeastern University Press, 1983), 362.

[18]John Buchanan, *The Road to Guilford Courthouse: The American Revolution in the Carolinas* (New York: John Wiley & Sons, Inc., 1997), 107.

[19]Ibid., 108-109.

[20]Ibid., 110.

[21]Ibid.

[22]Edgar, 73.

[23] Ibid.

[24] Ibid., 73-74.

[25] Ibid., 75-77.

[26] Ibid., 80-82.

[27] Ibid., 83-85.

[28] Ibid., 86.

[29] Morrill, 86.

[30] Ibid., 90.

[31] Ibid., 92.

[32] Ibid., 94.

[33] Ibid., 90.

[34] Ibid., 98.

[35] Ibid.

[36] Craig L. Symonds, *A Battlefield Atlas of the American Revolution* (Mount Pleasant, South Carolina: The Nautical & Aviation Publishing Company of America, 1986), 89.

[37] Morrill, 103.

[38] Hank Messick, *King's Mountain: The Epic of the Blue Ridge "Mountain Men" in the American Revolution* (Boston: Little, Brown and Company, 1976), 92.

[39] Morrill, 109.

[40] Ibid.

[41] Ibid.

[42] Buchanan, 233.

[43] Hibbert, 283.

[44] Morrill, 110.

[45] Ibid., 111.

[46]Henry Steele Commager and Richard B. Morris, eds., *The Spirit of Seventy Six: The Story of the American Revolution as Told by Participants* (New York: Da Capo Press, 1995), 1148-1149.

[47]William B. Willcox, *Portrait of a General: Sir Henry Clinton in the War of Independence* (New York: Alfred A. Knopf, 1962), 228.

[48]Ibid., 226.

CHAPTER 5

GREENE'S CAMPAIGN

The fourth factor that contributed to the failure of British strategy in the south was patriot General Nathanael Greene's campaign in 1780 and 1781. This chapter examines Greene's use of mobile warfare against Cornwallis's army. Next, it explores Greene's effectiveness in rallying the support of local leaders. Following that, this chapter analyzes his use of patriot militias against British forces. Additionally, it examines Greene's battles with the British at Cowpens and Guilford Courthouse and Cornwallis's withdrawal from the backcountry in April 1781. Lastly, it surveys Greene's final battles to destroy British backcountry garrisons during the second half of 1781.

On 14 October 1780, General George Washington convinced Congress to accept his nomination of General Nathanael Greene to command the Southern Department. Greene was a Rhode Islander who had never been farther south than Maryland. He brought important leadership and administrative skills to the command. Greene achieved a decisive victory against the British in the south through superior strategy. Cornwallis and his army permanently abandoned the backcountry less than five months after Greene's arrival in the south.

Greene was born to a middle class Quaker family in Potowomut, Rhode Island on 27 July 1742. His father was the spiritual leader of the surrounding East Greenwich Quaker community. He taught his son to glorify God by living an exemplary, sober, and useful life. Greene was an avid reader who devoured Euclid, Locke, and Swift. He also suffered from asthma. A childhood knee injury developed into a limp that stayed with him throughout his life.

In 1770, Greene moved to Coventry, Rhode Island and took charge of the family ironworks. The business manufactured chains, anchors, and other items used in shipping. It was here that Greene began to develop his exceptional administrative skills. He also displayed a talent for detailed planning and problem solving. One of Greene's staff officers later wrote, "No man was more familiarized to dispassionate and minute research than was General Greene."[1]

In 1774, Greene's religious community expelled him for volunteering for the Rhode Island militia. Greene's superiors quickly recognized his talent and promoted him to brigadier general. Greene met Washington in July 1775 and the two men established a close personal relationship that lasted throughout the war. Washington's aide wrote that Greene "is beyond doubt a first-rate military genius, and one in whose opinions the General places the utmost confidence."[2]

On 17 April 1776, Greene assumed responsibility for the defense of Long Island, New York. He participated in every major battle that Washington fought over the next three years. Greene crossed the Delaware River with Washington on 25 December 1776 and commanded troops in the patriot victory at Trenton, New Jersey. He spent the winter of 1777 with Washington at Valley Forge, Pennsylvania and the winter of 1778 with him at Morristown, New Jersey. Greene also faced Cornwallis while commanding troops at three northern battlefields: Brandywine, Germantown, and Monmouth Court House.

During the winter of 1777, Washington's army was close to starvation. General Thomas Mifflin was Washington's quartermaster general. He was responsible for providing for the army's logistical support and had clearly failed in his duties. On 25 February 1778, Washington removed Mifflin from his post and installed Greene as quartermaster general. Greene still hoped for a command position and had no desire to

serve as quartermaster general. He wrote to his brother, "No one has ever heard of a

quartermaster in history."[3] Greene also expressed his disappointment in his new position

directly to Washington. He wrote, "There is a great difference between being raised to an

office and descending to one which is my case."[4]

However, Greene was a professional officer. He accepted his new position and

immersed himself in his duties. His primary responsibility was the complicated task of

securing and transporting supplies to sustain the army in the field. Greene oversaw a staff

of about 3,000 men including deputy quartermasters, wagon masters, auditors, and clerks.

His effective administration soon yielded results. Under Greene, the quartermaster

department built a series of supply depots and roads in New Jersey and Pennsylvania. It

also built boats and wagons to transport supplies across the Delaware River and along the

northern roads. These projects dramatically improved the army's mobility. General

William Moultrie wrote that Greene's "military abilities, his active spirit, his great

resources when reduced to difficulties in the field, his having been quarter-master general

. . . all these qualities combined together rendered him a proper officer to collect and to

organize an army that was broken up and dispersed."[5]

On 23 October 1780, Greene met with Washington at Preakness, New York.

Washington informed him that Lieutenant Colonel Henry "Light Horse Harry" Lee and

his superb mounted Legion would be assigned to his command. This was crucial because

Greene intended to maximize his use of cavalry in the south. Greene's strategy was to

emphasize mobility, harass British forces, and avoid decisive engagement. Greene wrote that he planned to make Lee's Legion the core of a "flying army of about eight hundred horse and one thousand infantry."[6]

Greene decided to adopt the partisan tactics that southern militia commanders such as Francis Marion, Thomas Sumter, and Andrew Pickens had used effectively throughout the summer of 1780. Washington approved this strategy. Greene knew the British were undermanned in the south. He planned to force Cornwallis to choose between defending his backcountry garrisons and maneuvering against the patriot army in the field. If Cornwallis chose to defend his garrisons, Greene would attack the vulnerable British supply trains and isolate the backcountry garrisons. If Cornwallis chose to maneuver, Greene would withdraw and force Cornwallis to pursue him until Greene gained the advantage.

Greene was aware that the south contained numerous rivers. He believed that his success would be based on his army's ability to move fast, cross these rivers at will, and keep moving. Washington advised him to "direct particular attention to the boats."[7] Greene had learned the importance of careful logistical planning as Washington's quartermaster general. He would be equally attentive to logistics in the south.

On 2 December 1780, Greene joined the southern army at Charlotte, North Carolina. His force numbered 2,307 men. Of those present, 1,482 were fit for duty. Only 800 of the men were properly clothed and equipped. The core of Greene's army was the 949 remaining Maryland and Delaware Continentals that Baron Johannes de Kalb had marched south from Morristown, New Jersey seven months earlier.[8]

Cornwallis had badly beaten General Horatio Gates and the southern army four months earlier at the Battle of Camden. Congress had removed Gates from command and now replaced him with Greene. The army's morale was low. Greene wrote, "The appearance of the troops was wretched beyond description, and their distress, on account of provisions, was little less than their sufferings for want of clothing and other necessities."[9] Greene reported to Washington that many of his troops were "literally, naked; and a great part totally unfit for any kind of duty, and must remain so until clothing can be had from the northward."[10]

Greene was also disturbed by his army's lack of discipline. He wrote, "General Gates had lost the confidence of the officers, and the troops all their discipline, and they have been so addicted to plundering that they were a terror to the inhabitants."[11] Greene believed that the personal example of officers had a tremendous influence on soldiers. He wrote to Washington, "It has been my opinion for a long time that personal influence must supply the defects of civil constitution, but I have never been so fully convinced of it as on this journey."[12]

Greene was determined to restore discipline. He ordered his provost marshal to arrest a deserter and convened a court martial to try the soldier. The court found the soldier guilty of desertion and sentenced him to death. Greene ordered the entire army assembled and had the soldier hanged in front of the formation. His message was clear. Discipline improved immediately. One soldier reflected the army's mood towards its new commander: "New lords, new laws."[13]

Greene also began planning for his army's logistical support. He ordered Lieutenant Colonel Edward Carrington to conduct a survey of the Dan River on North Carolina's northern border. On 1 December 1780, Greene wrote to General Edward Stevens, "Lt Co Carrington is exploring the Dan River . . . and I want you to appoint a good and intelligent officer . . . to explore carefully the [Yadkin] River, the Depth of Water, the Current, and the Rocks, and every other obstruction that will impede the Business of Transportation."[14] Greene sent detailed instructions to Carrington:

> I . . . wish you to have forwarded . . . 500 felling Axes, 5888 Pair Horse Shoes, and if you found the Dan River navigable agreeable to your Expectations, half a Ton of Boat nails for constructing the batteaus [boats]. Let those come forward as soon as possible. One Third of the nails to be deposited on the Roanoke at the most convenient Place for building the batteaus, and the rest come on to Salisbury. . . . It will be well for you to consult with a good Shipwright the tools that will be necessary for Building about 100 large batteaus, and to take measures for having them forwarded without Loss of Time. Without Tools we can do nothing, and none are to be got in this Country, not even a common felling Axe.[15]

Greene demanded discipline and professionalism from his men. This proved to be an important factor in his victory over Cornwallis. Soldiers on both sides in the south tended to mistreat civilians and steal property. Commanders who enforced discipline were more likely to gain the support of the local people than those who permitted random violence and abuse. Greene understood that it was on this basis, as much as traditional battles, that the war in the south would be won or lost.

Greene's engagement with local leaders also contributed to his success. Cornwallis made similar attempts, but they proved largely unsuccessful. Greene believed that it was essential to reestablish civilian government in the south. He knew that the British had scattered the state assemblies and that a state of anarchy existed in the backcountry. Greene encouraged local leaders to reestablish law and order as soon as possible. He wrote to John Wilkinson, "I can think of nothing better made for the State [Georgia] to adopt to regulate its internal policies or secure itself from further ravages of the enimy than to form a Council to consist of five or seven of the most considerable charactors in the State whose orders should have the force of laws."[16]

Vigilantism was rampant throughout the south at this time. Backcountry dwellers frequently banded together and formed raiding parties to settle vendettas or dispense frontier justice. Greene urged Georgia Governor John Martin to prohibit civilians in his state from taking revenge on loyalists for past abuses. Greene realized that widespread reprisals against loyalists would lead to continued chaos and that this threatened to undermine the legitimacy of the patriot cause.

Unlike Greene, Martin was sympathetic to his citizens' desire for revenge. He wrote to Greene, "Nature would not be nature could it immediately forget injuries like those which impressions are only to be erased by time." Greene had no patience for Martin's view. He wrote back, "You say that nature would not be nature if you forgave them [the loyalists]--legislators should follow policy, not their own private resentments. A man in a legislative capacity is not at liberty to consult his private feelings in determining upon measures but how they will affect the interests of his Country."[17] Martin accepted Greene's advice and allowed Georgia loyalists to return to their homes without fear of reprisal.

Greene understood the importance of civil-military relations in war. He made every effort to convince rebel leaders not to repeat the British pattern of abuse and plunder against the local people. Greene worked tirelessly to rally the local people for the rebellion. In a remarkable role reversal, Greene essentially adopted Lord Germain's strategy of rallying the populace to achieve military victory. Unlike Cornwallis, Greene believed that gaining the support of the people was crucial to success. He wrote that engaging the British in battle without appealing to the local people for support would be counterproductive. Greene described this pure military approach as "making bricks without straw"--simply ineffective.[18]

Greene paid a great deal of attention to local rebel militia commanders. He realized that his army was not strong enough to challenge the British alone. In December 1780, Cornwallis was located at Winnsborough, South Carolina with 2,500 troops. Greene's base at Charlotte, North Carolina was about 90 miles north of Cornwallis's winter camp. On 4 December, Greene sent a letter to militia Colonel Francis Marion. He asked Marion to cooperate with him against the British:

> I have not the Honor of your Acquaintance but am no Stranger to your Character and merit. Untill a more permanent Army can be collected than is in the field at present, we must endeavor to keep up a partizan war and preserve the tide of sentiment among the People as much as possible in our Favour. . . . At present I am badly off for Intelligence. It is of the highest Importance that I get the earliest Information of any [British] Reinforcements which arrive at Charlestown or leave the Town to join Lord Cornwallis. I wish you therefore to fix some Plan for procuring such information and for conveying it to me with all possible Dispatch.[19]

Greene recognized the value of Marion's experience. In late December, he sent Lieutenant Colonel Henry Lee with 300 troops southeast along the Pee Dee River to join Marion. They planned to attack British wagon trains and harass British troops. On 28 December, Lee and Marion attacked the British garrison at Georgetown, South Carolina and captured the fort's commander. Next, they turned northwest and attacked the British garrison at Fort Watson. These raids produced the effect that Greene had hoped for. They forced Cornwallis to commit extra troops to protect his supply convoys traveling through the backcountry. The attacks also demonstrated Greene's flexibility. He was able to effectively combine his regular troops with local militia to harass the British.

In December 1780, Greene made a bold decision. He disregarded the traditional military view that a commander must never divide his forces when faced with a numerically superior enemy. On 16 December, he marched out of Charlotte with two-thirds of his army and established a new base at Cheraw, South Carolina. Greene's new camp was 70 miles southeast of Charlotte and closer to the coast.

Greene placed the remainder of his army under the command of Brigadier General Daniel Morgan. Morgan was one of the most talented patriot commanders of the war. In 1777, he had fought with Gates in New York against Burgoyne's army at Freeman's Farm and Bemis Heights. Morgan came out of retirement to serve Gates again in the south. Greene gave Morgan 320 of his Maryland and Delaware Continentals, 200 Virginia riflemen, and 100 dragoons under the command of Colonel William Washington. He also arranged for more local militia to join Morgan. General Andrew Pickens brought in 350 troops from South Carolina and General William Davidson arrived with 120 from North Carolina.

On 20 December, Morgan marched his force out of Charlotte and headed west towards King's Mountain. Greene wrote that he wanted Morgan "to give protection to that part of the country and spirit up the people, to annoy the enemy in the quarter." However, "should the enemy move in force towards the Pedee [River], where this army will take a position, you will move in such direction as to enable you to join me if necessary."[20]

Greene's plan was to pressure Cornwallis by threatening the British garrisons at Camden, Ninety-six, and Augusta. He wanted to force Cornwallis to abandon his safe winter camp at Winnsborough and expose his army to attack. Greene wrote:

77

It makes the most of my inferior force, for it compels my adversary to divide his, and holds him in doubt as to his line of conduct. He cannot leave Morgan behind him to come at me, or his posts at Ninety-six and Augusta would be exposed. And he cannot chase Morgan far, or prosecute his views upon Virginia while I can have the whole country open before me. I am as near to Charleston as he is, and as near Hillsborough as I was at Charlotte; so that I am in no danger of being cut off from my reinforcements.[21]

Cornwallis quickly responded to Greene's maneuver. He ordered General Alexander Leslie to reinforce the British garrison at Charleston with 1,000 troops of the 82nd and 84th Regiments. He also directed Leslie to reinforce him at Winnsborough with 1,500 additional troops. Those troops marched from the coast northwest towards Winnsborough in early January 1781. Cornwallis would have preferred to wait for Leslie's arrival before beginning his pursuit of Greene's army. However, he believed that he could not afford to wait. Morgan's movement through the backcountry was having the effect on Cornwallis that Greene desired. Cornwallis believed that Morgan's troops were a serious threat to his garrison at Ninety-six. Therefore, he decided to send Lieutenant Colonel Banastre Tarleton to protect the outpost.

During the first week of January 1781, Cornwallis ordered Tarleton to track down Morgan. Tarleton left Winnsborough with a 1,100-man force made up of 550 dragoons of the British Legion, the 249-man first battalion of the 71st Regiment, 200 men from the Seventh Regiment, 50 men from the 17th Light Dragoons, and two light artillery pieces called "grasshoppers."[22] Loyalist spies reported that Morgan was threatening the British outpost at Fort Williams, only fifteen miles northeast of Ninety-six. Cornwallis wrote to Tarleton, "If Morgan is still at Williams's, or anywhere within your reach, I should wish you push him to the utmost."[23] He also ordered Tarleton "to endeavor to strike a blow at General Morgan, & at all events oblige him to repass the Broad [River]."[24]

By dividing his army, Cornwallis had reacted exactly as Greene hoped he would. Tarleton's departure from Winnsborough increased the vulnerability of British supply lines and reduced Cornwallis's ability to concentrate his army. While Tarleton pursued Morgan northwest towards North Carolina, Cornwallis marched north along the Broad River with the rest of his army. Cornwallis's plan was to place his forces between Morgan and Greene's columns and destroy Greene's army. Cornwallis based his plan on the assumption that Tarleton would defeat Morgan and that he could march faster than Greene. Both of these assumptions proved to be false.[25]

Morgan's presence in the backcountry was a powerful temptation to Cornwallis to go on the offensive. Morgan's threat to Ninety-six reinforced Cornwallis's view that pursuing rebel forces was the key to victory in the south. Cornwallis was not convinced that Lord Germain's strategy of rallying the local populace would lead to victory. Cornwallis believed that he could defeat the southern rebellion if only he could destroy Greene's army like he had destroyed Gates's army at Camden.

In late 1780, Germain made a stunning strategic reversal. He now seemed to accept Cornwallis's view that destroying Greene's army would lead to British victory in the south. Germain wrote to Cornwallis, "I impatiently expect to hear of your further Progress. . . . I have not the least doubt, from your Lordship's vigorous and alert Movements, the whole Country South of Delaware will be restored to the King's Obedience in the Course of the Campaign."[26]

This was a complete break with Germain's original strategy which he described the previous year: "The great point to be wished for, is that the inhabitants of some considerable colony were so far reclaimed to their duty, that the revival of the British

79

Constitution, and the free operation of the laws, might without prejudice be permitted amongst them." In this way "a little political management, would with ease bring about what will never be effected by mere force."[27] By supporting Cornwallis's invasion of North Carolina and his pursuit of Greene's army, Germain had abandoned his support for "political management" in favor of military power.

Cornwallis's victory at Camden probably played a key role in changing Germain's view on strategy in the south. Both Germain and Cornwallis now seemed to agree that the best way to defeat the southern rebellion was to pursue Greene's army. However, they had unknowingly played into Greene's hand.

On 7 January 1781, Cornwallis marched his army out of its winter camp at Winnsborough. He headed north along the Broad River towards King's Mountain. Cornwallis moved slowly and hoped that Leslie would join him from the south with his reinforcements. Cornwallis was supremely confident that Tarleton and his Legion would destroy Morgan's force near Ninety-six. He wrote, "The . . . quality of the corps (of about eleven hundred men) under Lieutenant-Colonel Tarleton's command, and his great superiority in cavalry, left him no room to doubt of the most brilliant success."[28] Greene sent Morgan a note from Cheraw, "Colonel Tarleton is said to be on his way to pay you a visit. I doubt not but he will have a decent reception and a proper dismission."[29]

On 16 January, Morgan's scouts informed him that Tarleton was less than ten miles south of his position and riding fast. Morgan decided to turn and face the British commander. The local people called the place that Morgan chose Hannah's Cowpens. It was an area of open fields and sparse woods that local farmers used to graze their cattle.

A trail named Mill Gap Road ran southeast to northwest through the center of the battlefield.

Morgan decided to fight there because he had few other choices. The battlefield was close to the North Carolina border and only six miles south of the spot where the Broad River made a 90-degree turn from north-south to east-west. Morgan realized that if he did not stop and face Tarleton at Cowpens, he risked being caught between Tarleton and Cornwallis while crossing the Broad River. He also hoped to use Cowpens as a convenient gathering spot to attract more local rebel militia before the coming battle.

Morgan developed his battle plan carefully (see figure 2). He arranged his troops in three lines facing southeast towards Tarleton's line of advance along Mill Gap Road. Morgan placed each line higher on the gradually sloping ground of Cowpens. This forced the British to walk continuously uphill as they advanced against the rebels. Morgan's first line was made up of sharpshooters. The second line was Pickens's South Carolina militia. Morgan ordered Pickens to fire three volleys and withdraw. The third line was the Maryland and Delaware Continentals and the Virginia militia under the command of Colonel John Eager Howard. Morgan placed William Washington's cavalry behind the crest of the hill as a reserve.

At 7:00 A.M. on 17 January 1781, Tarleton arrived at the battlefield and arranged his troops into battle lines. He placed his infantry in the center and his dragoons on his flanks. Morgan's first line began shooting British officers as soon as Tarleton advanced. As Tarleton continued, Pickens's militia fired their three volleys. This stunned the British regulars. Tarleton ordered his dragoons to charge on his right flank to support the infantry. However, Washington's cavalry also charged from behind the crest of the hill

81

and routed Tarleton's dragoons. Now, Tarleton's infantry approached Morgan's third line. Howard's troops fired in volleys and charged. Almost simultaneously, Pickens's militia charged on the British left and Washington's cavalry charged on the right. This combined attack overwhelmed the British and Tarleton abandoned the field. The battle had lasted only one hour.

The Battle of Cowpens ruined the British Legion. It also ended Tarleton's reputation for invincibility. Cowpens was a disaster for the British just as Camden had been a disaster for the Americans. Tarleton lost 110 killed and 712 captured. This was a shocking 86 percent of his 1,100-man force. The rebels also captured a good deal of valuable British equipment. This included Tarleton's two light artillery "grasshoppers," 35 wagons, 100 horses, 800 muskets, a portable blacksmith's forge, and two regimental flags.[30] Morgan lost 12 killed and 60 wounded.[31] He wrote, "I was desirous to have a Stroke at Tarlton--my wishes are Gratified, & I have Given him a devil of a whiping."[32]

Morgan's victory stunned Cornwallis. He was determined to pursue Morgan and free the British prisoners. Leslie finally joined Cornwallis in mid-January and brought in 1,530 reinforcements. These included General Charles O'Hara's brigade and the German Bose Regiment. This brought Cornwallis's army to about 2,300 troops. Fortunately for Greene, Morgan pushed his troops relentlessly northward and marched 100 miles in five days. On 22 January, Morgan crossed the Catawba River ahead of Cornwallis.

Cornwallis now made a fateful decision. He wanted to transform his army into a light force that could match the impressive mobility of Greene's army. To accomplish this, Cornwallis decided to destroy his own supply wagons. He ordered all the army's wagons burned during the last week of January at Ramsour's Mill, North Carolina.

Cornwallis allowed only those vehicles carrying ammunition, medical supplies, and salt to be spared. This was a huge gamble. It was also in direct contravention of routine British military procedure. Later events demonstrated that this was a serious error. General O'Hara wrote:

> In this situation, without baggage, necessaries, or provisions of any sort for officer or soldier, in the most barren, inhospitable, unhealthy part of North America, opposed to the most savage, inveterate, perfidious, cruel enemy, with zeal and bayonets only, it was resolved to follow Greene's army to the end of the world.[33]

When Greene learned that Cornwallis had burned his supplies, he proclaimed, "Then, he is ours!"[34] Greene understood that Cornwallis had given up the ability to remain in the field for very long. The British would not be able to devote troops or resources to rallying the local populace, recruiting loyalists, or reinforcing their backcountry garrisons. Cornwallis would have to focus solely on achieving a decisive victory over Greene's army before his troops starved or ran out of ammunition. Greene described Cornwallis's gamble as a "mad scheme of pushing through the country."[35] Patriot Lewis Morris Jr. wrote, "The army was evidently the object of the enemy, and while we can keep that together the country can never be conquered--disperse it, and the people are subjugated."[36]

On 8 February 1781, Morgan and Greene rejoined their two columns at Guilford Courthouse, North Carolina. Greene now had about 2,000 troops in his army. He gathered his officers to discuss strategy and decided to continue pushing north towards Virginia. Greene knew that Cornwallis's supply lines now stretched over 200 miles to Charleston. He also knew that the British troops were becoming increasingly exhausted. Greene decided to continue to wear the British down since Cornwallis had clearly committed to pursuing him at all costs. Unfortunately for Greene, Morgan suffered from a painful back condition and left the army to recover in Virginia at this point. Greene wrote, "Great generals are scarce--there are few Morgans to be found."[37]

On 13 and 14 February, Greene took his army north across the Dan River and safely into Virginia. The army crossed the river in the boats that Greene had ordered Lieutenant Colonel Edward Carrington to build two months earlier. Greene's skill in logistical planning had now paid off. General Washington's guidance to him four months earlier to "direct particular attention to the boats" now seemed prescient. Cornwallis had no boats and was forced to withdraw to Hillsborough, North Carolina.

Greene took advantage of his brief stay in Virginia to resupply his army. He obtained fresh horses for Henry Lee's troops. Lee wrote, "The consequence was, the British dragoons were mounted upon small, weak horses: those of the Legion on stout, active horses."[38] Hundreds of new recruits joined Greene's army in Virginia. Colonel William Campbell brought in 400 Virginia riflemen and General Edward Stevens arrived with 700 Virginia militia.

In early March, Greene's army crossed back over the Dan River and into North Carolina. Greene continued to avoid battle with Cornwallis. On 10 March, he sent a note to Virginia Governor Thomas Jefferson. Greene explained that he would continue to avoid the British until he had the advantage. He wrote, "Hitherto I have been obliged to practice that by finesse which I dare not attempt by force. . . . Nothing shall hurry me into a Measure that is not Suggested by prudence or connects not with it the interest of the southern department."[39]

On 11 March, Greene dramatically increased the size of his army. General Robert Lawson arrived with 1,200 Virginia militia. Generals Thomas Eaton and John Butler brought in 1,000 North Carolina militia and 530 Virginia Continentals. This gave Greene about 4,400 troops.

By early March, Cornwallis had lost about 400 troops to death, injury, disease, and desertion. In addition, his supply situation had become desperate and his men were approaching the limits of their endurance. Cornwallis's army stood at about 1,950 men. Greene realized that he now held a numerical superiority over Cornwallis and the moment that he had been waiting for had arrived. Greene wrote, "Our force being now much more considerable than it had been and upon a more permanent footing, I took the determination to giving the enemy battle without loss of time and made the necessary dispositions accordingly."[40]

On 14 March, Greene's army returned to the village of Guilford Courthouse, North Carolina and prepared for battle. Greene chose this location to fight because he was familiar with the ground. He had surveyed the area with Morgan when the army camped there the month before. The battlefield was made up of open fields separated by densely wooded hillsides. Split rail fences outlined the fields. The 100-person village of Guilford Courthouse sat on the northern edge. The New Garden Road ran from northeast to southwest through the length of the battlefield. Little Horsepen Creek ran from west to east along the southwestern edge.

At Guilford Courthouse, Greene adopted Morgan's tactics from Cowpens (see figure 3). He arranged his army in three successive battle lines facing southwest. The New Garden Road bisected his formations. Greene made the 1,000 North Carolina militia under Generals Eaton and Butler his first line. He placed them behind an open field on the edge of the battlefield with the woods to their backs. Their task was to fire three volleys and withdraw. Greene placed two artillery pieces under Captain Anthony

Singleton in the center of this line. He placed Lee's Legion of 75 cavalry to the left and

Colonel William Washington's 90 dragoons to the right.

Greene placed his second line in thick woods 400 yards behind the first line. The

second line was made up of General Lawson's 1,200-man Virginia militia brigade.

Greene placed his third line 500 yards behind the second line at the crest of a small hill.

This last line was made up of Greene's 1,400 Continentals from Virginia, Maryland, and

Delaware.

Greene was less skillful than Morgan in arranging his troops. At Cowpens, the

battlefield was open and the troops in each battle line could see the line to their front. At

Guilford Courthouse, the battlefield was much larger and the woods prevented the lines

from supporting each other. The woods also prevented Greene from seeing the entire

battlefield as Morgan had at Cowpens. Greene also failed to establish a reserve. This

reduced his ability to react quickly to tactical changes. These observations are not

surprising since Greene was not a superb tactician. His genius lay in strategic thought and

logistical planning.

At 1:30 P.M. on 15 March 1781, Cornwallis's army marched out of the woods on

the southwestern edge of the battlefield. Cornwallis immediately arranged his 1,924

troops for a massive frontal assault. He placed them in two successive 1,000-yard lines

and gave the order to advance. Greene's first line fired when the British approached

within 150 yards. At 50 yards, the British charged and the North Carolina militia fled

through the woods to their rear. The British lines fractured when they met Greene's second line in the woods. The Virginia militia fought well and reduced the strength of the British units as they continued towards Greene's third line.

Cornwallis's army had now fought two battles and still faced fresh rebel troops. The British emerged from the woods and saw Greene's third line of 1,400 Continentals waiting. The Continentals fired and counterattacked as the British approached. Washington's cavalry also charged against the rear of the British lines. British and rebel lines intermixed and the soldiers fought hand to hand with bayonets and sabers. Cornwallis saw that his lines were collapsing and ordered his artillery to fire into the troops at close range. This desperate act killed scores of British and rebel troops and stopped Greene's counterattack. Greene was now convinced that he had achieved all that was possible that day. He ordered his units to withdraw from the battlefield at 3:30 P.M. The battle had lasted two hours.

The Battle of Guilford Courthouse was a narrow tactical victory for Cornwallis because he retained possession of the battlefield. It was also a major strategic victory for Greene. Patriot losses were 79 killed and 184 wounded. This was a six percent casualty rate for Greene's 4,400-man army. British losses were 93 killed, 413 wounded, and 26 missing. In one battle, Greene had destroyed a stunning 27 percent of Cornwallis's 1,924-man force.[41] It was now reduced to about 1,400 troops and could not remain in the field. Cornwallis had ruined his army.

Greene realized that he had severely damaged his British foe. He wrote, "I have never felt an easy moment since the enemy crossed the Catawba until since the defeat of the 15th, but now I am perfectly easy, being persuaded it is out of the enemies power to do us any great injury."[42] Greene was correct. Cornwallis now had no choice but to withdraw his army to safety.

On 18 March, Cornwallis marched his exhausted army east to Cross Creek, North Carolina. He wrote to Clinton in New York, "With a third of my army sick and wounded . . . the remainder worn down with fatigue, I thought it was time to look for some place of rest and refitment."[43] However, Cornwallis found only hostile inhabitants and few supplies at Cross Creek. He decided to continue east and sought refuge near the coast at Wilmington, North Carolina.

On 7 April 1781, Cornwallis's army arrived at Wilmington. Lord Germain's strategy of rallying the local populace for British rule was in ruins. Clinton had made it clear to Cornwallis that his first priority was the security of Charleston and South Carolina. Cornwallis had disregarded this order and marched his army across North Carolina in pursuit of Greene. The British met disaster at Cowpens and Guilford Courthouse. Cornwallis expressed his frustration with the results of his campaign in a letter to General William Phillips, "I assure you that I am quite tired of marching about the country in quest of adventures."[44]

In Wilmington, Cornwallis struggled to develop a new plan. He now believed that the key to British victory was to abandon the south, abandon New York, and "bring our whole force into Virginia; we then have a stake to fight for, and a successful battle may give us America."[45] On 25 April, Cornwallis marched his army out of Wilmington and headed north towards Virginia. Six months later he surrendered his entire army to General George Washington at Yorktown.

Following Cornwallis's withdrawal to the coast, Greene decided to turn south and attack the remaining British garrisons. He wrote to Washington, "I am determined to carry the war immediately into South Carolina."[46] Greene made good on his pledge. He again teamed Lee's Legion with Francis Marion's partisans. On 23 April, they captured Fort Watson, South Carolina. Simultaneously, Greene marched against Camden with 1,500 men.

On 25 April, Greene fought Colonel Francis Rawdon and his 900 troops at the Battle of Hobkirk's Hill. Following Cornwallis's departure for Virginia, Rawdon had assumed command of all remaining British and loyalist forces in the south. Rawdon fought skillfully at Hobkirk's Hill and forced Greene to withdraw. However, Rawdon abandoned his vulnerable position at Camden after the battle. On 10 May, he withdrew his troops to Charleston. Greene had turned another tactical defeat into strategic victory. He wrote, "There are few generals that has run oftener, or more lustily than I have done. But I have taken care not to run too far."[47]

On 8 September 1781, Greene faced Lieutenant Colonel Alexander Stewart at the Battle of Eutaw Springs. This was the final battle between British and rebel forces in the south. Greene had 2,400 troops. He attacked Stewart and his 2,000 troops at the British camp at Eutaw Springs. The camp was located 50 miles northwest of Charleston. The patriots fought well and pursued the British through their camp and beyond it. However, Greene's exhausted troops stopped in the middle of the attack to loot the British camp of food and equipment. This gave Stewart a chance to counterattack and Greene withdrew from the field.

It was another tactical victory for the British and another strategic victory for the patriots. Stewart soon abandoned the backcountry. He withdrew all remaining British troops in the south to Wilmington, Charleston, and Savannah. Although southern loyalists and patriots continued fighting throughout 1781 and 1782, the British never again ventured out of their coastal bases. Stewart's withdrawal to the coast signaled the final failure of Lord Germain's strategy of rallying the support of the local populace to defeat the rebellion.

General Greene's campaign contributed significantly to the failure of British strategy in the south. His use of mobile warfare against Cornwallis's army was exceptional. Greene was not a brilliant tactician, but he turned a series of tactical defeats into strategic victory. His skill at rallying the support of local leaders and militia commanders was crucial to his success. After Cornwallis's disaster at Guilford Courthouse, Greene forced the British to abandon the south by continuing his campaign into South Carolina. Henry Lee described the result: "The conquered states were regained, and our exiled countrymen were restored to their deserted homes--sweet rewards of our toil and peril."[48]

---

[1]Theodore Thayer, *Nathanael Greene: Strategist of the American Revolution* (New York: Twayne Publishers, 1960), 296.

[2]Elswyth Thane, *The Fighting Quaker: Nathanael Greene* (New York: Aeonian Press, Inc., 1977), 62.

[3]Dan L. Morrill, *Southern Campaigns of the American Revolution* (Baltimore: The Nautical & Aviation Publishing Company of America, 1993), 115.

[4]Ibid.

[5]Richard Wheeler, *The Voices of 1776: The Story of the American Revolution in the Words of Those Who Were There* (New York: Penguin Books, 1991), 358.

[6]Mildred F. Treacy, *Prelude to Yorktown: The Southern Campaign of Nathanael Greene, 1780-81* (Chapel Hill: University of North Carolina Press, 1963), 58.

[7]Ibid., 59

[8]John Buchanan, *The Road to Guilford Courthouse: The American Revolution in the Carolinas* (New York: John Wiley & Sons, Inc., 1997), 288.

[9]Morrill, 118.

[10]Ibid.

[11]Henry Steele Commager and Richard B. Morris, eds., *The Spirit of Seventy Six: The Story of the American Revolution as Told by Participants* (New York: Da Capo Press, 1995), 1152.

[12]Thayer, 289.

[13]Morrill, 119.

[14]Buchanan, 288.

[15]Ibid., 289.

[16]Mark A. Clodfelter, "Between Virtue and Necessity: Nathanael Greene and the Conduct of Civil-Military Relations in the South, 1780-82," *Military Affairs* 52 (October 1988): 171.

[17]Ibid., 172.

[18]Ibid., 174.

[19]Buchanan, 290.

[20]Ibid., 296.

[21]John S. Pancake, *This Destructive War: The British Campaign in the Carolinas, 1780-1782* (Tuscaloosa: University of Alabama Press, 1985), 131.

[22]Buchanan, 309.

[23]Commager and Morris, 1155.

[24]Pancake, 132.

[25]Ibid., 133.

[26]Buchanan, 307.

[27]Pancake, 12.

[28]Wheeler, 360.

[29]George F. Scheer and Hugh F. Rankin, *Rebels and Redcoats: The American Revolution Through the Eyes of Those Who Fought and Lived It* (New York: Da Capo Press, 1987), 427.

[30]Buchanan, 326.

[31]Don Higginbotham, *The War of American Independence: Military Attitudes, Policies, and Practice, 1763-1789* (Boston: Northeastern University Press, 1983), 367.

[32]Buchanan, 329.

[33]Morrill, 138.

[34]Ibid., 140.

[35]Ibid., 139.

[36]Commager and Morris, 1162.

[37]Morrill, 143.

[38]Pancake, 174.

[39]Buchanan, 368.

[40]Commager and Morris, 1163-1164.

[41]Morrill, 157.

[42]Buchanan, 382.

[43]Ibid.

[44]Ibid., 383.

[45]Ibid.

[46]Morrill, 159.

[47]Ibid., 161.

[48]Ibid., 169.

CHAPTER 6

CONCLUSION

The purpose of this research is to discover the factors that led to the failure of British strategy in the American south during 1780 and 1781. The thesis of this paper is that these factors were: (1) a false British assumption of loyalist support among the southern populace, (2) British application of self-defeating political and military policies, (3) British failure to deploy sufficient forces to control the territory and protect southern loyalists, and (4) patriot General Nathanael Greene's campaign against British forces.

Lord George Germain's strategy for the south was to rally the support of the local populace for British rule. His goal was to influence loyalist militias to rise up in great numbers and defeat the rebels. He also wanted these loyalists to provide aid and support to British forces throughout the backcountry. Germain wrote to General Henry Clinton that he wanted to use British military power in the south to persuade the Americans to permit "the revival of the British Constitution and the free operation of the laws . . . amongst them." He believed that the rebellion could only be defeated by "political management," never "by mere force." However, Germain failed to convince his military commanders of the wisdom of this political approach to the conflict.[1]

The first factor that led to the failure of Lord Germain's strategy was the false British assumption of widespread loyalist support in the south. In 1778, Germain came under extraordinary pressure from George III and Prime Minister Frederick North to develop a new strategy for the war in America. A number of British political and military leaders played a role in influencing Germain's belief in the southern loyalists. Germain was perfectly willing to accept the reports of former royal governors who wrote that "if a proper number of troops were in possession of Charleston . . . the whole inhabitants of both provinces would soon come in and submit."[2] Later events demonstrated that this was not true.

Since Germain based his strategy on this false assumption, the plan was severely flawed at inception. British soldiers learned through bitter experience that the southern patriots were far from ready to "come in and submit" in 1780 and 1781. General Charles O'Hara described the patriots as a "most savage, inveterate, perfidious, cruel enemy." General Charles Cornwallis faced a southern population that was increasingly opposed to British rule rather than the loyalist majority that Germain expected.[3]

The second factor that led to the failure of Lord Germain's strategy was the application of self-defeating political and military policies. Clinton's decision not to reestablish civilian government in the south was a serious error. His failure to link British military power to local civilian authority undermined the legitimacy of Cornwallis's campaign. Clinton's decision to compel paroled rebels to take loyalty oaths was another error. Many of the southerners felt no obligation to honor the oaths because they had taken them under duress. Others viewed the policy as one more example of British tyranny and rejoined the rebellion.

British and loyalist atrocities against southern rebels and civilians were also extremely counterproductive. These atrocities included torture, summary executions, church burnings, and theft of property. These practices fueled southern resistance to British rule. British policy on slavery and Indians also contributed to the failure of Germain's strategy. Many southerners lived in constant fear of a widespread slave rebellion. Cornwallis's policy of using escaped slaves as loyalist militia outraged the

94

local populace and handed rebel leaders a convenient propaganda victory. British support for the Cherokee, Chickasaw, and Creek played into southern fear of Indian attack. These policies and practices provided local patriot leaders many opportunities to hold British leaders up to the local populace as convenient hate symbols.

The third factor that led to the failure of Lord Germain's strategy was the British failure to deploy sufficient troops to control the south and protect southern loyalists. In 1780 and 1781, Great Britain deployed forces around the world to fight a global war with France, Spain, and Holland. The massive manpower demands of this conflict severely limited the available troops that Germain and Clinton had to send Cornwallis. In the south, Cornwallis attempted to control an area of 141,000 square miles and a population of 507,000 people with 4,000 troops. In June 1780, Clinton established a series of backcountry garrisons throughout the south including Camden, Ninety-six, and Augusta. When Cornwallis assumed command later that month, he used up three-fourths of his 4,000-man army simply manning these remote bases.

Throughout 1780 and 1781, patriot militia raided Cornwallis's supply convoys. They capitalized on British weakness in numbers by attacking the patrols that ran from Cornwallis's coastal bases to his backcountry garrisons. The most striking example of the patriot militia's effectiveness was their slaughter of Major Patrick Ferguson's loyalists at the Battle of King's Mountain on 7 October 1780. The rebels demonstrated that they could strike the British at will by surrounding and destroying Cornwallis's loyalists in the backcountry. The British disaster at King's Mountain illustrated the futility of Cornwallis's attempt to conquer the south with a few thousand troops.

The fourth factor that led to the failure of Lord Germain's strategy was General Nathanael Greene's campaign against British forces. Greene's use of mobile warfare against the British was exceptional. Greene disregarded conventional wisdom and baited Cornwallis into pursuing him by dividing his army into two columns and threatening the British backcountry garrisons. In March 1781, Cornwallis's army grew steadily weaker from fatigue and disease while Greene doubled the size of his army. On 15 March 1781, Greene finally faced Cornwallis at the Battle of Guilford Courthouse and destroyed over one-fourth of Cornwallis's army in two hours. Cornwallis abandoned his invasion of North Carolina and withdrew to the coast.

Greene had turned a narrow tactical defeat into a major strategic victory through careful operational and logistical planning. However, he was not content with this victory and he continued his campaign into South Carolina. After the Battle of Eutaw Springs on 8 September 1781, the remaining British troops in the south withdrew to their coastal bases at Wilmington, Charleston, and Savannah. They never ventured into the interior again.

The failure of British strategy in the south in 1780 and 1781 was due to a false assumption of loyalist support, self-defeating political and military policies, the failure to deploy sufficient troops, and General Nathanael Greene's campaign. Clinton reflected on the failure of the southern strategy in a letter to Germain on 18 July 1781. He wrote, "For, if as I have often before suggested the good will of the inhabitants is absolutely requisite to retain a country after we have conquered it, I fear it will be some time before we can recover the confidence of those in Carolina."[4] As Clinton feared, the British never regained the confidence of those few loyalists who remained in the south. The British withdrawal to the coast in September 1781 signaled the final defeat of Lord Germain's

strategy of rallying the southern populace for British rule.

---

[1]John S. Pancake, *This Destructive War: The British Campaign in the Carolinas, 1780-1782* (Tuscaloosa: University of Alabama Press, 1985), 12.

[2]Dan L. Morrill, *Southern Campaigns of the American Revolution* (Baltimore: The Nautical & Aviation Publishing Company of America, 1993), 39.

[3]Ibid., 139.

[4]William B. Willcox, *Portrait of a General: Sir Henry Clinton in the War of Independence* (New York: Alfred A. Knopf, 1962), 309.

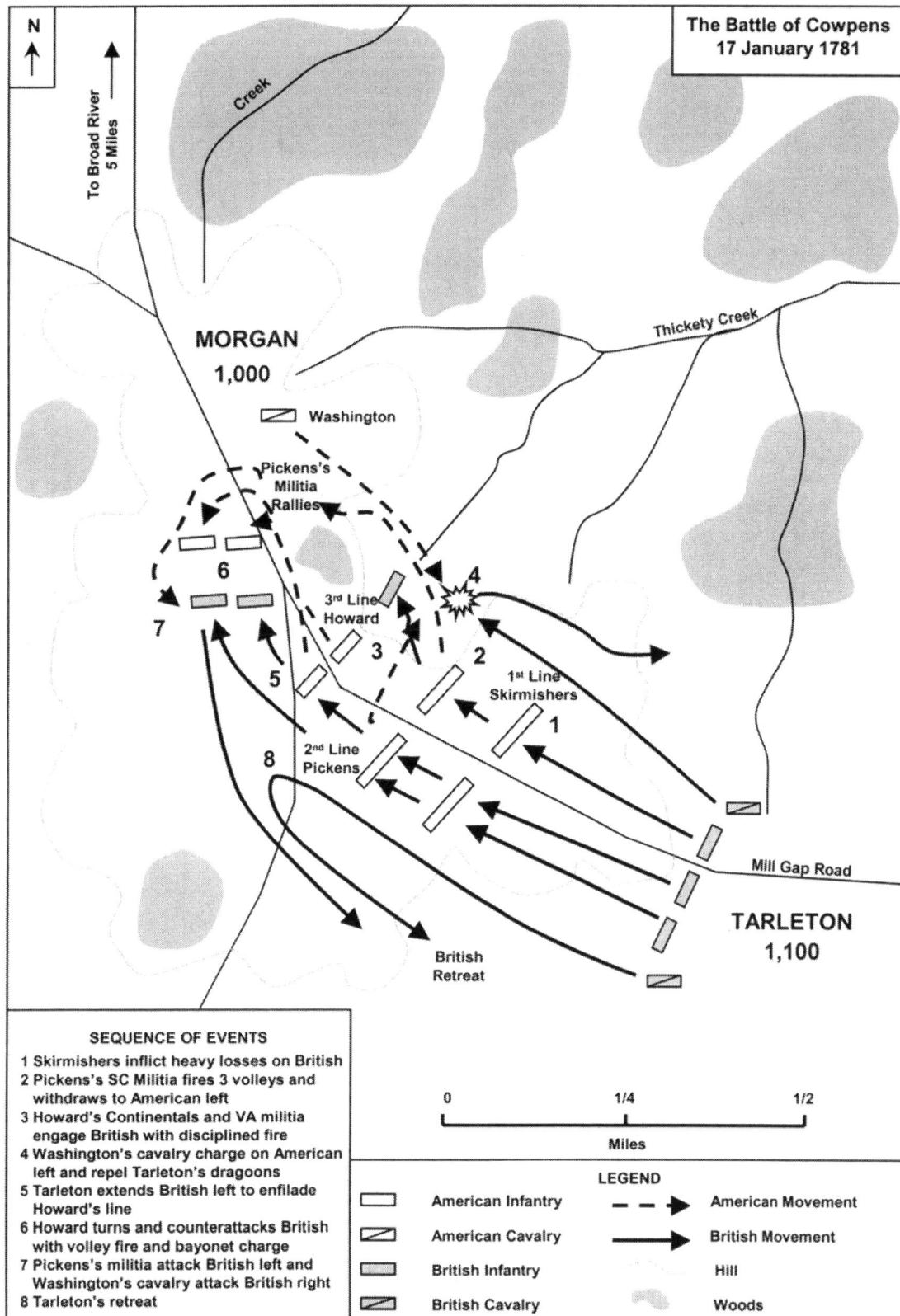

N

To Broad River 5 Miles

Creek

**The Battle of Cowpens
17 January 1781**

Thickety Creek

**MORGAN
1,000**

Washington

Pickens's
Militia
Rallies

6

7

3rd Line
Howard

4

5

3

2

1st Line
Skirmishers

1

2nd Line
Pickens

8

Mill Gap Road

**TARLETON
1,100**

British
Retreat

SEQUENCE OF EVENTS
1 Skirmishers inflict heavy losses on British
2 Pickens's SC Militia fires 3 volleys and
  withdraws to American left
3 Howard's Continentals and VA militia
  engage British with disciplined fire
4 Washington's cavalry charge on American
  left and repel Tarleton's dragoons
5 Tarleton extends British left to enfilade
  Howard's line
6 Howard turns and counterattacks British
  with volley fire and bayonet charge
7 Pickens's militia attack British left and
  Washington's cavalry attack British right
8 Tarleton's retreat

0   1/4   1/2

Miles

LEGEND

▭	American Infantry	---▶	American Movement
▱	American Cavalry	━▶	British Movement
▨	British Infantry		Hill
▨	British Cavalry		Woods

Figure 2.   The Battle of Cowpens

99

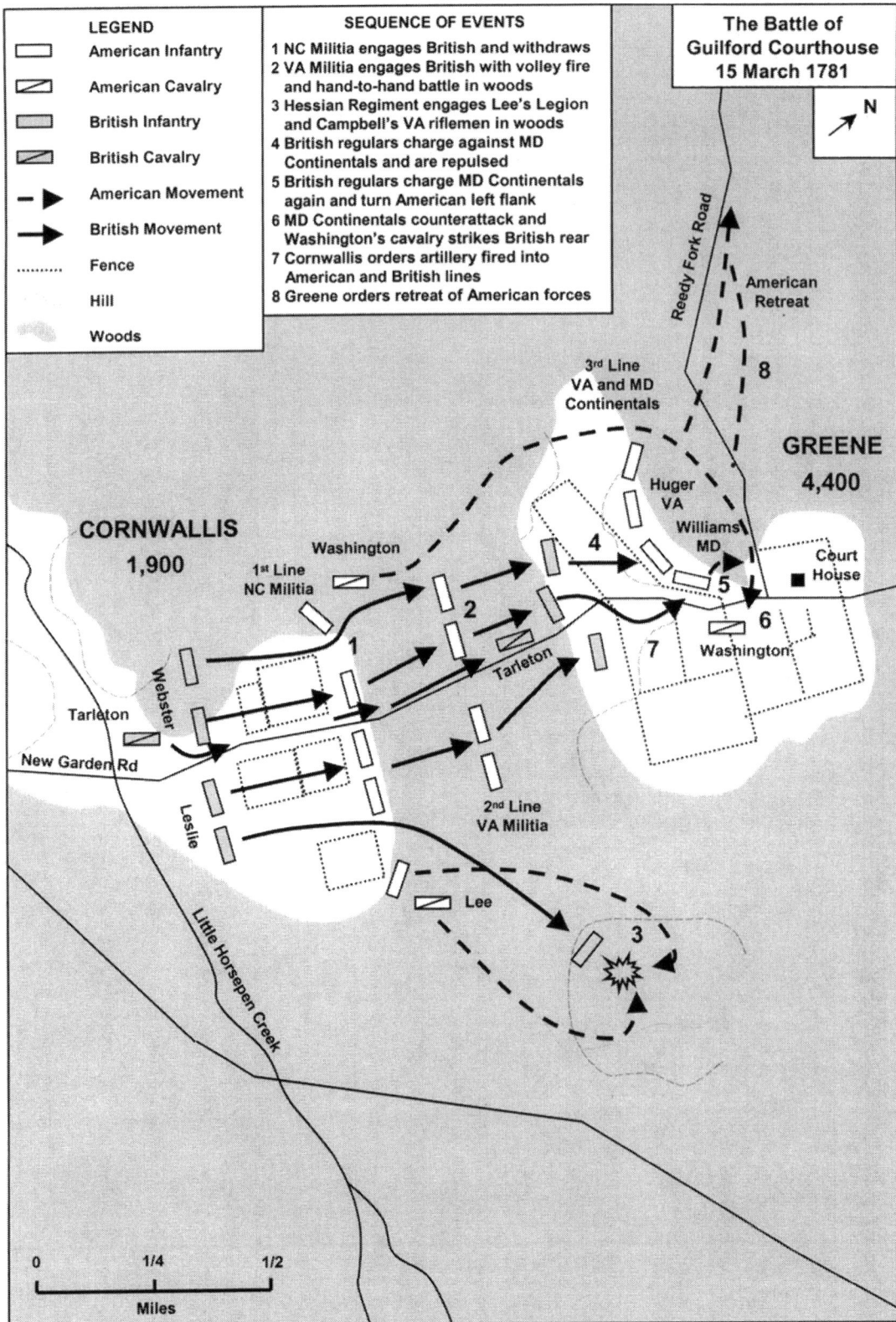

Figure 3. The Battle of Guilford Courthouse

BIBLIOGRAPHY

Books

Boatner, Mark M., III. *Encyclopedia of the American Revolution*. Mechanicsburg, Pennsylvania: Stackpole Books, 1994.

Bowler, R. Arthur. *Logistics and the Failure of the British Army in America, 1775-1783*. Princeton: Princeton University Press, 1975

Buchanan, John. *The Road to Guilford Courthouse*: *The American Revolution in the Carolinas*. New York: John Wiley and Sons, Inc., 1997.

Commager, Henry Steele, and Richard B. Morris, eds. *The Spirit of Seventy Six: The Story of the American Revolution as Told by Participants*. New York: Da Capo Press, 1995.

Edgar, Walter B. *Partisans and Redcoats: The Southern Conflict that Turned the Tide of the American Revolution*. New York: HarperCollins, 2003.

Hibbert, Christopher. *Redcoats and Rebels: The American Revolution Through British Eyes*. New York: W. W. Norton and Company, 2002.

Higginbotham, Don. *The War of American Independence: Military Attitudes, Policies, and Practice, 1763-1789*. Boston: Northeastern University Press, 1983.

Lambert, Robert S. *South Carolina Loyalists in the American Revolution*. Columbia, South Carolina: University of South Carolina Press, 1987.

Lumpkin, Henry. *From Savannah to Yorktown: The American Revolution in the South*. Lincoln, Nebraska: toExcel Press, 2000.

Mackesy, Piers. *The War for America, 1775-1783*. Lincoln, Nebraska: University of Nebraska Press, 1993.

Messick, Hank. *King's Mountain: The Epic of the Blue Ridge "Mountain Men" in the American Revolution*. Boston: Little, Brown and Company, 1976.

Morrill, Dan L. *Southern Campaigns of the American Revolution*. Baltimore: The Nautical and Aviation Publishing Company of America, 1993.

O' Donnell, James H. III. *Southern Indians in the American Revolution*. Knoxville: University of Tennessee Press, 1972.

Nadelhaft, Jerome J. *Disorders of War: The Revolution in South Carolina*. Orono, Maine: University of Maine Press, 1981.

Pancake, John S. *This Destructive War: The British Campaign in the Carolinas, 1780-1782*. Tuscaloosa: University of Alabama Press, 1985.

Quarles, Benjamin. *The Negro in the American Revolution*. Chapel Hill: University of North Carolina Press, 1961.

Scheer, George F., and Hugh F. Rankin, eds. *Rebels and Redcoats: The American Revolution Through the Eyes of Those Who Fought and Lived It*. New York: Da Capo Press, 1987.

Sherman, William Thomas. *Calendar and Record of the Revolutionary War in the South: 1780-1781*. Seattle: William Thomas Sherman, 2003.

Symonds, Craig L. *A Battlefield Atlas of the American Revolution*. Mount Pleasant, South Carolina: The Nautical and Aviation Publishing Company of America, 1986.

Thane, Elswyth. *The Fighting Quaker: Nathanael Greene*. New York: Hawthorn Books, Inc., 1972.

Thayer, Theodore. *Nathanael Greene: Strategist of the American Revolution*. New York: Twayne Publishers, 1960.

Treacy, Mildred F. *Prelude to Yorktown: The Southern Campaign of Nathanael Greene, 1780-81*. Chapel Hill: University of North Carolina Press, 1963.

Wheeler, Richard. *The Voices of 1776: The Story of the American Revolution in the Words of Those Who Were There*. New York: Penguin Books, 1991.

Wickwire, Franklin, and Mary Wickwire. *Cornwallis: The American Adventure*. Boston: Houghton Mifflin Company, 1970.

Willcox, William B., ed. *The American Rebellion: Sir Henry Clinton's Narrative of His Campaigns, 1775-1782, with an Appendix of Original Documents*. New Haven: Yale University Press, 1954.

Willcox, William B. *Portrait of a General: Sir Henry Clinton in the War of Independence*. New York: Alfred A. Knopf, 1962.

Periodicals

Clodfelter, Mark A. "Between Virtue and Necessity: Nathanael Greene and the Conduct of Civil-Military Relations in the South, 1780-1782." *Military Affairs* 52, no. 4 (October 1988): 169-175.

Conway, Stephen. "'The great mischief Complain'd of': Reflections on the Misconduct of British Soldiers in the Revolutionary War." *William and Mary Quarterly* 47, no. 3 (July 1990): 370-390.

Endy, Melvin B., Jr. "Just War, Holy War, and Millennialism in Revolutionary America." *William and Mary Quarterly* 42, no. 1 (January 1985): 3-25.

Power, J. Tracy. "The Virtue of Humanity Was Totally Forgot: Buford's Massacre, May 29, 1780." *South Carolina Historical Magazine* 93, no. 1 (January 1992): 5-14.

11751147R00060

Printed in Great Britain
by Amazon.co.uk, Ltd.,
Marston Gate.